Gandolfini

Gandolfini

The Real Life of the Man Who Made Tony Soprano

DAN BISCHOFF

SCRIBE

Melbourne • London

Scribe Publication Pty Ltd

18–20 Edward St, Brunswick, Victoria 3056, Australia
50A Kingsway Place, Sans Walk, London, EC1R 0LU, United Kingdom

Originally published by St. Martin's Press, USA, 2014
This edition first published by Scribe, UK, 2014

Printed and bound by CPI Group (UK) Ltd, Croydon, CR0 4YY

National Library of Australia
Cataloguing-in-Publication entry

Bischoff, Dan, author.

Gandolfini: the real life of the man who made Tony Soprano /
Dan Bischoff.

9781922247322 (UK paperback)
9781922072863 (e-book)

1. Gandolfini, James. 2. Sopranos (Television program). 3. Actors–United States–Biography. 4. Television actors and actresses–United States–Biography. 5. Italian Americans–Biography.

791.45028092

scribepublications.com.au
scribepublications.co.uk

For my mother,
Rose Mary Maher Bischoff

Contents

Acknowledgments

I undertook this book almost overnight, and it would never have seen the light of day without the kind ministrations of my agent, Scott Mendel, whose inspiration started it all. My editor, Elizabeth Beier, provided crucial enthusiasm for the topic and has always been understanding about every deadline, while Michelle Richter made sure I crossed every elastic line on time.

This book would also not be here without the attention of Meryl Gross, production editor at St. Martin's, or the help provided by publicist Katie Bassel and marketing experts Erin Cox and Angie Giammarino. Steven Seighman designed the interior, and the cover was put together by Rob Grom.

This book was not written with the official cooperation of the Gandolfini family and reflects my conclusions, not theirs. Yet the loyalty James Gandolfini engendered in those who knew him, like high school teacher Ann Comarato, fellow student Donna Mancinelli, and Park Ridge mayor Don Ruschman, tells us a lot about his character. Mark Di Ionno's sharp understanding of New Jersey's social landscape was as important as his assessment of his college buddy's nature, and few have a subtler feeling for the artist his friend would become than T. J. Foderaro. Skylar Frederick, the graduating editor of *The Daily Targum*, the campus newspaper at Rutgers University, helped check stories for me in campus files, a courtesy for which I'm very grateful. The professional acumen of actor Roger Bart, and of course that of Gandolfini's first professional acting teacher Kathryn Gately, were invaluable; and Gandolfini's coach, collaborators, and friends Harold Guskin and Sandra Jennings, were as generous with their experience as anyone could be. The man many people called Jim's best friend, once a sportswriter for *The Daily Targum*, a fellow bouncer at the campus pub, a manager at Bell Labs, and ultimately an executive at Attaboy Films, Tom Richardson was an unfailing gentleman at every turn.

Susan Aston was part of Gandofini's personal and professional life longer than anyone, and her wry but sweet realism is the finest praise a subject could want.

Gandolfini's managers Mark Armstrong and Nancy Sanders were essential to telling the story of the actor's life in Hollywood, and Angela Tarantino of HBO was unfailingly helpful. Tony Sirico and his pal Al Giordano of Wounded Warriors care a great deal about their friend's commitment to the generation that came home from war without a G.I. Bill. And the thoughtful generosity of Nicole Holofcener and Michaël Roskam, the directors of Jim's two posthumous films, was very welcome. The work of so many fine journalists from Alan Sepinwall and Matt Zoller Seitz to Peter Biskind and Chris Heath informed every page. My colleagues at *The Star-Ledger*, in particular my editor Enrique Lavin and librarian Giovanna Pugliesi, extended a cooperative understanding for which I'll always be grateful.

More personally, I have to thank Marc Cooper and Natasha Vargas-Cooper, whose crucial help at a key moment made the book possible. Maria Laurino started me off with a characteristically perceptive analysis of Italian-Americans in New Jersey, her own specialty. I should close with the names of all those friends and colleagues whose support over the course of the book was important to me in more ways than I can describe here: Peter Kwong and Dušanka Miščević, Allen Barra and Jonelle Bonta, James and Pat Ridgeway, Chuck and Ires Wilbanks, Will Rosenthal, Emily Hubley, Martha Elson, Pate Skene, Willie Neuman, Andie Tucher, and so many more I'm surely being churlish to forget. My good friend Kevin Jon Klein, a playwright and professor of screenwriting at Catholic University, happily acted as a sounding board for many of the ideas presented here (so anything that's wrong is partly his fault).

Finally, my family, my sister, Kathy, and my brother, John, and of course my son, Boone, are the reasons this book was written. I hope they know how much I've always appreciated their support. My wife and fellow writer, Leslie Savan, who provided a second pair of eyes for every word you find here, knows for sure.

Gandolfini

1.

All Roads Lead to Rome

It was not unlike the way *The Sopranos* ended, in Holsten's ice cream parlor in Bloomfield, New Jersey: One minute Tony's changing the jukebox to Journey's "Don't Stop Believin'," waiting for his daughter, Meadow, to join the rest of the family for onion rings. And then, fade to black.

Only this time, the restaurant was in a five-star hotel in Rome, built on third-century Roman ruins across the street from a church Michelangelo designed for the last intact ancient *tepidarium*, in the Baths of Diocletian. James Gandolfini was in Italy with his son, Michael, on vacation. They'd arrived on the twelve-hour flight from Los Angeles the night before, and had just had "a beautiful day" sightseeing. Jim told friends he'd been looking forward to a "boys' trip," where he and Michael, thirteen, could explore their Italian heritage together—it was something Tony Soprano had said he wanted to do after touring Naples in the second season, let his kids see "all this stuff they come from."

In the afternoon, he took Michael to the Vatican. He bought a couple of rosaries for his sisters, blessed by Pope Francis and promising indulgences, the proceeds dedicated to the convent that works for Rome's poor. Then they went to the Musei Vaticani to see, among much else, the mummies and sarcophagi in the Ancient Egyptian galleries. They were photographed there standing between two illustrated coffin lids by a pair of American tourists from Philadelphia.

They left the Vatican in the middle of one of those Roman afternoons in June when the rooflines waver in the sun and the fountain spray evaporates before it hits the pool. They were waiting for James's sister Leta, who was arriving from Paris that night after meetings with her dress company, American Rag. They were going to enjoy a few days in the curving Boscolo Hotel Exedra on the Piazza della Repubblica until Jim made a scheduled appearance at the Taormina Film Fest in Sicily, where he'd do an appearance with an old castmate, Marisa Tomei.

It was just James and Michael that night in the hotel's outdoor restaurant, still trying to get past the jet lag and fall into sync with Italian time. They ate, lingered over drinks and dessert, and started drifting up to their room around 9:00 P.M.

And then, fade to black.

At least, that's how it felt to many. Michael found his father on the floor of the bathroom in their suite at around ten that night and called the desk for help. An emergency crew from the nearby Policlinico Umberto I was there in minutes; Gandolfini was still alive, even as they wheeled him, bare-chested and wrapped in a hotel blanket, out through the lobby. He died at the hospital of cardiac arrest, after continuous resuscitation efforts, forty minutes later. He was fifty-one years old.

At first, the world reacted the way so many had to the end of *The Sopranos*—with absolute shock. Then the cascade of regrets, well-wishes, and sorrow for an actor who made millions sympathize with a stone-cold killer for almost ten years, becoming part of the American family. Everyone expected many more years, and many more characters, each one subtly reshaping the working-class hero he'd become—such as *Enough Said,* a romantic comedy with Julia Louis-Dreyfus for Fox Searchlight, expected for 2014 (the company would put it into quick turnaround after Gandolfini's death), about a woman who falls in love with her friend's husband. Slowly, the realization sunk in that this fade-out meant something else—there would be no *Sopranos* movie.

Ever since "Don't Stop Believin'" went into its last verse in that Bloomfield ice cream parlor, every fan of *The Sopranos* had been asking when their favorite mob family would get its big-budget, *Godfather*-type, silver-screen treatment, as if that would somehow be better. Gandolfini had been asked about it just a few days before he took off for Rome, by a TMZ paparazzo on a Los Angeles sidewalk, and he'd answered that he had no idea. The only time, he said, he was sure it would get made was when "David Chase runs out of money."

Even that won't be enough to get it made now, because there is no *Sopranos* without Tony Soprano. James Gandolfini's creation, from 1999–2007, of the lugubrious mob boss with such mother problems that he starts seeing a female therapist, became one of the most indelibly mythic characters of American television. Tony was a kind of cross between Marlon Brando's Stanley Kowalski and Carroll O'Connor's Archie Bunker, a raging id of greed and lust who could make you laugh at the clumsiness of his surgically precise malapropisms. Tony was "with that Senator Sanitorium" on the issue of gay rights; he could be "prostate with grief"; revenge, he believed, was "like serving cold cuts."

And yet, Tony was not a buffoon. Or anyway, not just a buffoon. Something in the alchemy of Gandolfini's performance made Tony very real to millions of Americans and fans around the world. So real that James Gandolfini's death seemed as if it had happened to a neighbor, or a relative. His death was all in the family.

And at the same time, it was *Six Feet Under, Deadwood, The Shield, Mad Men, The Wire, Breaking Bad,* and *Justified.* James Gandolfini was one of those actors who changed the medium in which they performed. It's often said that he introduced an era of TV antiheroes. What he definitely did was show us a bad man who hurt other people out of his own vulnerabilities. As America went around serving cold cuts to the rest of the world after 9/11 (the Twin Towers fell within sight of some of the scenes in *The Sopranos'* famous opening credits), and its rusting middle-class economy barreled toward decline and collapse, that theme seemed to take on an importance far beyond TV itself.

To understand James Gandolfini, it's important to know that all roads lead to Rome—but they start in New Jersey. Where your birthplace can be an exit ramp.

"A large number of actors and musicians are from [New Jersey]," Gandolfini once told *The New York Times.* "We are overrepresented in the culture. You have a blue-collar, middle-class sensibility right next to one of the greatest cities in the world, which can make for some interesting creative impulses."

Like, maybe, the impulse to take a baseball bat to polite culture, or the impulse to grab pleasure hard, or just the impulse to give in to your impulses. People forget, but it's no accident that Roy Lichtenstein invented Pop Art while he was teaching at Rutgers, or that Bruce Springsteen was mourning the death of the American Dream before the media across the river realized it was sick. The state's greatest poet, William Carlos Williams, was an obstetrician serving poor, immigrant, working-class families in Paterson from a horse and buggy.

And Snooki is a real person.

The tight braiding of banality and art was *The Sopranos'* signature. At a time when most scripted TV shows were still shot on soundstages in Los Angeles or gussied up with exotic locales, *The Sopranos* featured video shoots on city street corners, in the Meadowlands swamp, at mall parking lots—it looked like it was shot out of your car window. When the audience watched Tony's crew threaten to toss a persuadable civilian off the bridge over the Great Falls in Paterson, folks around the country saw a dramatically dark and craggy waterfall, but Jerseyans saw a place they'd all trooped through on school day-trips.

The show's creator, David Chase, is himself a son of New Jersey, with his own complicated relationship to his Italian heritage and his home state. Back in the late 1970s, when Chase was starting out, he produced a genial but often topical private-eye show starring James Garner called *The Rockford Files.* He wrote an episode titled "Just a Coupla Guys," about aspiring Italian-American mobsters from New Jersey who would stand out like black socks on a beach in L.A. It said a lot, even then, about the sour state of mind his native state puts David Chase in.

The plot had Garner landing at Newark airport as a fellow passenger tells him how nice the city really is, that it's gotten an unfair rap. In short order, after getting off the plane, Rockford's watch, luggage, and rental car are stolen, and a little later the character is mugged on the street. The easy freedom of the California lifestyle and American abundance seem suspicious in a Jersey setting, like some kind of con. The germ of the mob comedy that *The Sopranos* would become was in a line spoken by the dead-eyed wannabe hitman (played by Greg Antonacci) to Garner: "I hate you guys with your convertibles and your cheeseburgers." The new suburbia was ruining America for the mob.

Native New Jerseyans have a sort of sad-sack, also-ran, second-rate phobia as their birthright, because they live on the wrong side of the river from Manhattan. It's a bit of a jinx, like the little raincloud over Al Capp's Joe Btfsplk. When David Chase finally got his mob comedy on the air at HBO, it was incredibly annoying that so many people assumed it was a knock-off of the Robert De Niro/Billy Crystal vehicle, *Analyze This*, which opened earlier the same year. Like *The Sopranos*, *Analyze This* was a comedy about a mob boss in therapy, only this time he's a New York kingpin who grows dependent on his nebbishy Jewish shrink and needs to consult him in moments of unexpected crisis.

Cue the laughing trombones. In real life, Chase's wife, Denise, had been telling him to make a movie about his tortured relationship with his Italian-American mother in Jersey for years. Chase had been steadily pitching the idea of an Italian mob boss trying to cope with his mom and suburban assimilation before HBO signed on, and before Harold Ramis got a green-light for *Analyze This*.

It's like a conspiracy: nobody from Jersey ever gets credit for nothin'. Especially if they're Italian.

And yet, they're proud of it. It's just the strangest thing, that New Jerseyans believe this wellspring of bitterness and disappointment allows them to see the truth clearer, unblinkingly, while the rest of the world goes around seeing blue skies and opportunity everywhere. It's a kind of moral superiority. A kind, of course, that is in no way dented by stealing your watch.

As *The Sopranos* took off and drew a global audience, the intertwining of fact and fiction became even tighter. Chase hired actors from an A-list of tri-state–area Italian-American actors who, over many years and many productions, had become a kind of repertory theater of big-city mobsters for Hollywood. But he hired a lot of near-amateur actors from Jersey as well, to add local color. Several of them happened to get arrested during the series, for misdemeanors and felonies. Assault, drug possession, insurance fraud, hiring someone to beat a man for not paying a debt, even second-degree murder charges were leveled against *Sopranos* actors. Robert Iler, who played A.J., Tony's son on the show, was arrested and pleaded guilty to mugging a pair of Brazilian tourists. The press loved these stories—it was life imitates art.

But the main claim *The Sopranos* laid to Jersey authenticity and art was Tony himself, or really, James Gandolfini. Like Tony, Gandolfini was born and raised in the Garden State. His father was born in Italy, outside of Milan, and his mother was born in New Jersey but raised near Naples. They spoke Italian in the home, though not to their kids.

Jim and his two sisters, Leta and Johanna, never learned Italian, but Jim said he could tell when his parents "were mad at me" in Italian.

His family had followed the great migration from Newark to the suburbs that began in the late 1950s, all the way out to Park Ridge, in Bergen County. James Joseph Gandolfini, Sr., was a World War II veteran, with a Purple Heart to show for it, despite his Italian birth. He became a bricklayer and cement mixer who wound up head custodian of Paramus Catholic High School. Jimmy Gandolfini's mother, Santa, was a school lunch lady. His father would set up loudspeakers outside the house every summer and mow the lawn in his boxers to the accompaniment of blaring Italian songs. "He was a real Guinea," his son recalled.

And maybe it was the vast conspiracy—against Italians from New Jersey, against big guys with big personalities, against the working class—that made Gandolfini reluctant to ever talk about this rich personal life, so intimately bound up with his greatest artistic creation, in public. He rarely gave interviews to the press.

"I'm not trying to be difficult," he told one of the few journalists he would open up to, *The Star-Ledger*'s Matt Zoller Seitz, in 1999. "It's not that I'm afraid to reveal personal stuff. . . . It's just that I really, genuinely don't see why people would find that sort of thing so interesting."

He'd interrupt journalists who asked about him by saying "Boriiiing!" and try to change the subject. For an actor who appeared so unguarded on the screen or stage, his reticence about his background seemed like a mystery.

And yet, he acknowledged several times that he'd made Tony up out of his own biography. "The character is a good fit," Gandolfini said. "Obviously, I'm not a mobster, and there's other aspects of the guy I'm not familiar with, like how comfortable he is with violence. But in most of the ways that count, I have to say, yeah—the guy is me."

How he got that across on the home screen was a private matter, however. Like a lot of serious dramatic actors, he hated the froufrou and flattery of publicity and promotion. That stuff seemed to eat away at his self-esteem, rather than buck it up (in that he was again like Brando, and a lot of other tough-guy male leads, including Robert Mitchum and Lee Marvin). There was something that kept him from wholeheartedly accepting his celebrity or the privileges it could command.

Well, some of them. The ones that weren't, you know, Jerseyan.

Vanity Fair once asked him about what it was like to go from being working class to international celebrity wealth (he left an estate valued in the press at anywhere from $6 million to $70 million at his death). Gandolfini mulled the question, hemmed and hawed. "Money is good! So I'm very happy about that," he announced at last. "All the fuss during *The Sopranos* really was pretty ridiculous. None of us expected it to last, and it lasted almost ten years. Honestly? I don't think I'm that different. I've lived in the same apartment for years. I've kept a lot of the same friends. I'm still grumpy and miserable. . . . But in a good way!"

It was as if, after thinking of himself as a struggling actor for so long, Gandolfini didn't want to lose touch with who he was. He did stay loyal to old Jersey friends, even as he started hanging out with the likes of Alec Baldwin and Brad Pitt. Friends like Tom Richardson, now an executive at Attaboy Films, Gandolfini's production company, and Mark Ohlstein, a chiropractor, and Vito Bellino, an ad executive for *The Ledger*. They'd hang out with each other and their families, go to the beach, and watch Rutgers football together.

Gandolfini did TV commercials for Rutgers' Scarlet Knights football team as *The Sopranos* was reaching the height of its popularity. In 2002, he got Michael Imperioli, who played his nephew, Christopher Moltisanti, on *The Sopranos*, to direct one that showed Richardson, Ohlstein, and Bellino coming out onto the field at the fifty-yard line, congratulating themselves on how Gandolfini's celebrity had gotten them "real close" to the action. They ask what it had cost him to get them there, and Gandolfini says, "Me? Nothing." A moment later they're shown holding the Scarlet Knight mascot costume, plus the two halves of the costume for his horse. Ohlstein looks into the camera and says, sarcastically, "Close. Real close."

Nobody escapes the Jersey curse—I don't care who they think they know.

Never hitting the top of your arc, always bumping against some invisible ceiling, is what Tony, and *The Sopranos,* was all about. James Gandolfini symbolized that inbred New Jersey pessimism, and made the rest of the world love him for it. Add a few more pounds and a hint of the anger and you've got Chris Christie, who may run for president in a few years, something I doubt anybody his size and temperament could have done before Tony Soprano.

Most of the planet lives with its nose against the glass today, looking, the way New Jersey looks across the river to Manhattan, at someone's more successful life somewhere on the other side of the screen. For white men of a certain age it's almost endemic. The paradox of James Gandolfini's life is that by expressing that feeling with frustrated passion, by making us care for the inarticulate longing of a very conflicted but common man, he was able to pass through the screen, move to Tribeca, become rich and famous—for about thirteen lucky years.

He didn't make it look easy. In fact, Gandolfini, who decided he wanted to be an actor as early as high school, made it look very hard—like labor, actually. As if carrying Tony Soprano around inside you was like hefting a hod of bricks.

On the set he'd hit himself, hard, in the back of the head, if he flubbed lines or missed his mark. As time went on the actor found it got more difficult to bring the same level of kinetic authenticity to the role. Sometimes he'd just hunker down in his Tribeca apartment and miss a whole shoot, only to show up the next day with gifts, like a masseuse for the crew, or some fabulous caterer for the lunch table. Once, after he'd landed a huge raise, he showed up and peeled off $33,000 apiece for everybody he saw, telling them, "Thanks for sticking with me."

Fellow actors did stick with him. They saw something special about his talent almost from the beginning. After he'd gotten his first real break, in the 1993 crime thriller *True Romance* (written by Quentin Tarantino), and developed the reputation as an actor with an absolutely fascinating emotional range, Gandolfini seemed oblivious. He would have an acting coach, Susan Aston, with him on nearly every set, something hotshot movie stars rarely do.

Aston met him in the eighties, when Gandolfini was working construction and as a bouncer in nightclubs in New York City. They became acting partners and friends. They met when they were both studying at Actor's Playhouse, a center for method acting, and specifically the Meisner technique. They worked together until she delivered a eulogy at his funeral at the Cathedral of St. John the Divine in New York City in June 2013.

Meisner's technique involves a series of interdependent exercises intended to use the actor's life experiences to obtain spontaneity and emotional coherence. It's a stage technique but, like all American method acting, it achieves

13

its greatest effects in film. Sanford Meisner developed his method in the 1940s after leaving Stella Adler and Lee Strasberg's Group Theatre in New York, which taught a variant of the Stanislavski system. Steve McQueen, Robert Duvall, Gregory Peck, James Caan, Jeff Bridges, Alec Baldwin, and James Franco have all been trained in the Meisner technique, and it is often described as intense and demanding. Some actors, often those who wash out, describe it as abusive and psychologically invasive.

In 2004, Gandolfini made an appearance on *Inside the Actors Studio*, a program on Bravo hosted by James Lipton, and gave the longest discussion in public he'd ever offered on acting as a profession.

"I remember one thing [an early acting teacher] did for me that got me to a new level was—I had such anger back then," Gandolfini said. "When you're young, a lot of people do, everybody does. You're pissed. And you're not sure why. . . . 'Cause you want to express something and you're not sure what it is. Something happened, I think [the acting teacher] told a partner to do something to me. And he did it, and I destroyed the place. Y'know, just all that crap they have onstage. And then she said, at the end of it—I remember my hands were bleeding a little bit and stuff, and the guy had left—and she said, 'See? Everybody's fine. Nobody's hurt. This is what you have to do. This is what people pay for. . . . They don't wanna see the guy next door. These are the things you need to be able to express, and control, work on the controlling part, and that's what you need to show.'"

The distinguishing mark of James Gandolfini as an actor was his ability to find sympathy for the devil within the characters he played without, somehow, suppressing the deviltry. He learned to let people glimpse the monster of his temper as an actor and it was thrilling, so real did the emotion seem.

There's a single, twelve-minute-long scene in *True Romance* in which Gandolfini viciously beats Patricia Arquette to get her to tell him where she's hidden the cocaine he wants. The scene—it took five days to shoot—is incredibly brutal. He pounds her face, throws her through a glass shower door, and repeatedly, gently, tells her why he is in complete control of the situation. Until, that is, she sets him on fire and kills him with his own shotgun.

That scene is almost a movie in itself, a journey of character discovery with an astonishing denouement. But what stands out is Gandolfini's thoughtful, almost playful attitude until the very end. The chilling way he clothes his anger in a slight smile, while not really hiding it at all. It's a virtual audition for the part of Tony Soprano.

The psychological tension necessary to maintain that characterization over several days of technical shooting was extraordinary, for both actors. They had to hit a balletic rhythm, and stay in character after several peaks and valleys of emotional intensity. The pressure on a film set can be intense—visitors, time limits, scheduling conflicts, all contribute to a hectic, distracting environment. Gandolfini's commitment to technique also demanded a complete immersion in the character to achieve his startling spontaneity.

That may be why, as Aston says, it became almost a standard part of the process for Gandolfini to try to quit every part he ever landed. And that's why Aston was there—to bring him back to the character. She'd be on the set, then go over the next day's script with him that night. And they could be long nights—union rules say an actor has to have twelve hours off after every full day, so starting times each succeeding day get pushed farther and farther back until you are filming in the wee hours. He had a bag of Meisnerian tricks—Gandolfini once told the press that if you need to do an angry scene, "don't sleep" for two or three days, or walk around with something sharp in your shoe—but his real secret was preparation. And a vivid imagination.

Star actors are well paid for what they do, so we needn't indulge in any false pity here. But many American method actors, especially men, begin to find trolling through such emotional depths increasingly difficult with time. A lot of entertainment doesn't require it, of course. But that can only add to your frustration with the job. If there is this very difficult thing that you do very well, but it is taxing to do and there isn't always a demand for it, you can develop a healthy contempt for the whole process. As Brando did, and Mitchum, too.

"It's a hard head to get into sometimes," Gandolfini told GQ. "I have a lot of fun at work too, don't get me wrong. I love the people I work with. But there are some days when you get to work and you're not angry enough, and you have to kind of get angrier and that's a little . . . when I was younger, it was much more accessible."

Maybe we can illustrate something about the Meisner technique, and method acting in general, with that always coyly self-referential production, *The Sopranos*. Toward the end of the series there's an episode where Tony is recovering from being shot in the stomach by Uncle Junior. He's worried about maintaining the respect of his crew in his weakened condition. He's tried to compensate by hiring a driver/bodyguard whose obvious muscles—he drives around in a wife-beater and desert camo pants—is part of his job description. So Tony nerves himself up to sucker punch his bodyguard in front of the whole mob family, knocks the guy down, kicks him, and storms into the bathroom.

There we see Tony lean over the sink, breathing heavily, and then suddenly vomit into the toilet. He returns to the sink, stares haggardly at himself in the mirror, and then breaks into a barely perceptible smile. He's let the mob get a glimpse of the monster again; he's created the impression he wanted. And then he vomits once more.

For Tony, the scene is about keeping control with a clever stratagem: he's intimidated the rest of the greedy sharks, and he's glad he's done it. But for Gandolfini, the scene is also a tribute to the Meisner technique. Giving us a glimpse of the monster is what actors do, too—as Gandolfini told the audience on *Inside the Actors Studio*, the best lesson he ever learned in acting school was that they don't come to see "the guy next door." Letting us glimpse the monster is what made him such a good actor—that sly little smile in the mirror recognizes that Jim's done it again, and he's proud of the effect.

But finding that monster, bringing him up and putting him on the screen in a way that seems entirely convincing, does not come without some psychic cost. That's the second vomit—the price you pay. Meisner preached using your personal history, your own sadness and pain, the real core of your own feelings, to create a convincing reality on stage or screen. James Gandolfini could bring up the authentic monster. But doing that for years can make you a physical wreck.

"Violent roles?" Gandolfini said, in 2010. "Yeah. That's all I got for a while. It's okay. I'm an angry guy. I'm like a sponge. You wring yourself out and then you have none of that left in you for a while. It can be a good thing that way. I'll do those parts again. It takes a toll though. Definitely takes a toll."

Acting is a skill that some of us have and others don't. And that skill can be improved with practice and discipline. But there's no question that how you look, your physical type, shapes the roles you're offered. When Gandolfini was auditioning for Tony Soprano, for example, he was sure the role would go to some "handsome George Clooney type, except Italian."

The contrast between Gandolfini's career and that of another Italian-American movie star who also happens to be from a roughly similar neighborhood in New Jersey—John Travolta—is interesting in this way (Travolta's dad, who lived in Englewood, sold Gandolfini's dad automobile tires). Travolta's big break came on TV too, on the sitcom *Welcome Back, Kotter* in 1975, when he was barely out of his teens. He's played handsome leading men all his life.

Gandolfini didn't get his first sizable role, in *True Romance*, until he was thirty-two; he didn't land his first lead role, as Tony, until he was almost thirty-nine (lucky for him the whole country, or at least its social conscience, seemed to be entering middle age at the same time). But it's not a career path that predominates in entertainment. And, as he told *Inside the Actors Studio*, you've simply "got to work with what you got"—and it can be a blessing. "I wouldn't have had the roles I've gotten if I looked like Peter Pan."

Of course, most of the people who make their living in front of a camera *do* look a little like Peter Pan. Looks and hype are twin pillars in the architecture of celebrity culture.

Beloved as he was, Gandolfini nonetheless stood out (though not alone, of course) in the lettuce-eating film community. A doctor who'd never treated him told the press after his death that he was "a heart attack waiting to happen." There were tweets after his death was announced calling him "fatty," followed by a backlash against the tweeters. The *New York Post* ran a cover story detailing his last meal in Rome: "Gandolfini guzzled four shots of rum, two piña coladas, and two beers at dinner with his son—while he chowed down on two orders of fried king prawns and a 'large portion' of foie gras, a hotel source in Rome said."

One of Gandolfini's first jobs in Manhattan was at an Upper East Side wine bar ("you could take home $100, $125 a night in tips there, and it helped if you knew your wine," a friend who worked with him says). He worked in restaurants, clubs, and bars, like a lot of actors do, for years before he landed his first big part on stage. One of his best friends from his Rutgers days was chef Mario Batali, who started out cooking in a New Brunswick restaurant where Jim worked the bar. Later on, the actor would be a regular at Batali's New York and L.A. restaurants, which specialize in Italian cuisine. The redheaded, portly Batali is also an expert in classical Italian cooking, and his ancestors go back more than a century in the West Coast Italian-American community.

Gandolfini didn't just serve time in the food-and-drink industry. While still in his midtwenties he was hired to manage Private Eyes, a big, high-tech, high-priced night-club on West Twenty-first Street in New York. He was good at his job, managing a "whole crew of bouncers," buying liquor, running the help staff. And managing the public, too. There's more than a little Manhattan bouncer in Tony Soprano and many of his film roles.

The caricature of the New Jersey good life—good food, drink, people, family—well, not everybody comes out of that looking like The Situation. New Jersey is often described as a "tribal" state, an archipelago of different ethnic cultures that persist even now. Among Italian-Americans who migrated westward along Bloomfield Avenue, away from Newark into the thinning ether of suburbia, the maintenance of the culture, and resistance to assimilation, is closely tied to family and food. *The Sopranos* devoted a whole episode to it.

That Gandolfini was part of that culture contributed to the authenticity he brought to the role of Tony. As an actor of surprising range, he could find an authenticity in all sorts of characters. After all, he's played a New York City mayor (*The Taking of Pelham 1 2 3*), an American general (*In the Loop*), even the director of the CIA (albeit the first Italian-American one, Leon Panetta, in *Zero Dark Thirty*). But many of the people who knew him well describe Gandolfini's life as a search for authenticity, both professionally and personally. That's why he tried to quit so often, because he feared he could not summon it; that's why his performances have such an unexpected impact when he brings it. The number of times he called "bullshit" on acting and Hollywood and publicity departments would almost fill a book itself. He was serious about what he did.

So there was no easy line on his life for the press. He had not constructed a pasteboard identity to go with the role of James Gandolfini that he tried to hawk the way so many young actors do.

Oh, he'd thought about it. One weekend when he was first starting to find his footing as an actor on the stage in New York, he went home for dinner with his parents and sisters, and asked them if they'd mind if he changed his name to "James Leather," so that fans wouldn't come knocking on the Gandolfini door.

"I said, 'If I get famous, it could be a pain in the ass.'" They seemed to be mulling it over as he got up to go to the bathroom. When he came back, they were all laughing hysterically at the idea that Jimmy Gandolfini will become famous. "So that's my family, you know?"

It's a common contradiction, the contrast between who you are and who you're playing. Gandolfini never completely lost that conflict, again like so many great method actors before him. It made him an acrobat in pain, always the best show under the tent. It also made him intensely private, reluctant to talk about himself, and so a bit of a mystery to his fans, who perhaps could be forgiven for calling him "Tony" when they met in person. Gandolfini as an actor seemed totally unguarded, but as a man, there were walls.

He made his name playing a series of thinking hit-men: Virgil in *True Romance;* Ben Pinkwater, a seemingly mild-mannered insurance salesman who turns out to be a psychotically violent Russian mobster, in *Terminal Velocity;* a gentle leg-breaker and bodyguard for gangsters in *Get Shorty;* a mob enforcer who turns on his partner, played by Alec Baldwin, in *The Juror.* And, of course, Tony Soprano. A little mystery probably helped the gregarious party animal get over in those roles. It certainly helped deliver the shock of Tony Soprano's near reality TV presence for a decade.

Gandolfini became very good at hinting at depths of sadness and vulnerability that were left mostly to the imagination. When he won his third Emmy as a leading dramatic actor for *The Sopranos,* he gave a short, heartfelt acceptance speech that included a mention of Lynne Jacobson, whom viewers may have assumed was a college acting teacher, or an old friend who kept him in school, or something. It wasn't until almost a year later, in an interview, that he acknowledged publicly that she had been his first love while they were both at Rutgers, and she'd died in a car accident when he was still a junior.

Jim always said he wanted to play people "like my mom and dad." He complained about superhero movies, which have largely taken over Hollywood, helping to shift serious drama over to cable (a cultural reversal Gandolfini is often credited with achieving almost single-handedly). Movies were all so fake. Gandolfini wanted to be real.

So did *The Sopranos*. It was art imitates life imitates art: Bringing the American bromance of gangster movies to modern suburban life, where the church has lost credibility, the neighborhood is scattered, and family is attenuated to the point of transparency. Where did the real begin and the fake start? What *is* real anyway?

The series became a long tease about those questions. And at first the final episode's fade to black seemed like an evasive answer. "When I first saw the ending, I said, 'What the fuck?'" Gandolfini told *Vanity Fair* the year before he died. "I mean, after all I went through, all this death, and then it's over like that?"

Then he woke up the next morning.

"But after I had a day to sleep, I just sat there and said, 'That's perfect.'"

2.

Park Ridge Italians

When James Gandolfini was eleven years old, in 1972, Paramount released *The Godfather*, and the gap between the rich and the poor in America was the smallest it has ever been in its history.

The Godfather was the capstone for a long series of hit gangster movies, beginning with Edward G. Robinson's *Little Caesar* in 1931 and continuing, at regular intervals, through *The Sopranos*. For a long period *The Godfather* was the highest grossing film of all time. In a barbershop-mirror way, the world of *The Godfather* has replaced the reality of organized crime for many fans, and real gangsters now model themselves on its characters—on *The Sopranos*, we overhear thugs in tracksuits discussing the film's finer points as if they were Roger Ebert.

Director Francis Ford Coppola hit upon the idea of turning the gangster into an analogue of the American capitalist, forced to adapt to survive, constantly changing with the times and the culture, and thereby slowly "losing the family." It was a love letter to the stubborn ethnic cultures of the Northeast, which were being worn away by suburban mobility, rock 'n' roll, and the general prosperity of the 1970s.

Of course, the Corleones were a *New York* crime family, and their idea of the suburbs, at least in Coppola's imagination, was a fieldstone estate in Lake Tahoe. As the series progressed we got to see them not only kill their fellow Italian-American competitors but threaten movie producers and United States senators, successfully suborn the grand jury process and defy Congress. They were captains of industry, building the new world, convening corporate board meetings (only, instead of energy or railroads, they oversaw illegal booze, gambling, prostitution, and the labor rackets).

It was a little over the top.

The reality for Italian-Americans was less operatic than that. When Italians began immigrating to the United States in large numbers (between 1880 and 1920 some four million Italians recorded entry to the United States, more than any other ethnic group over a period lasting almost half a century), many of them settled in cheap housing in port cities. Factory work, dock labor, and construction jobs were mainstays.

Today, Little Italy in Manhattan is a tourist-trap vestige, a few blocks under constant threat of being swallowed by a burgeoning Chinatown. But back then the tenements were crowded with recent immigrants. They helped found similar concentrations in cities all around the region. Many of the new arrivals were uneducated peasants from the south of Italy, traditionally the poorest section of the boot, and they dreamed of moving out of the cities.

"The majority of Italians came after Garibaldi united Italy, and one of the outcomes of unification was compulsory education," says Maria Laurino, who published a book in 2000, *Were You Always an Italian?*, about the woes of New Jersey Italian-American assimilation. David Chase read Laurino's book, blurbed the paperback, and then distributed it among *The Sopranos'* scriptwriters. Laurino was raised in the upscale suburb of Short Hills, New Jersey, but her father came from neighboring Millburn, which had a large concentration of southern Italians. Laurino, whose brother Robert is now an Essex County prosecutor, is descended from emigrants from Basilicata and Avellino; David Chase's mother's people come from Avellino, too.

"Most of them had been peasants for many, many generations," Laurino says, "people who worked the soil. The dream was a little land in the country. But the idea of a son who'd be better educated than his father, who would not respect his father because he knew more—that was anathema to them. So that was one of the reasons why they moved to the United States in huge numbers. Compulsory education had been in place for years [in the United States], but they were already here when they found out."

Many of these immigrants complained of American prejudice, of being asked to repeat themselves because of their accent or being followed around in department stores. More than one Italian-American has told me something like, "My grandfather never thought he was white."

In New Jersey, the earliest concentrations of Italians were in Newark, first in the city near the factories and warehouses, and then in Vailsburg, on the city's western border, and in mill towns like Paterson. In *The Sopranos*, Tony's mother and father are buried in a graveyard in Vailsburg. The inner-belt suburbs offered factory work and tedious finishing jobs that could be done in the home (independent Italian garment workers, usually women, sewed "piecework"—"piece-a-work"—that paid per item of clothing completed long after the postwar boom began to fade).

New Jersey Italians began their long march toward that little piece of land in the countryside along Bloomfield Avenue, which runs roughly northwest out of the city toward the Caldwells (Tony Soprano's McMansion was in North Caldwell). Bloomfield Avenue became known as "Guinea Gulch," lined with Italian-American homes and businesses. Vesuvio, Artie Bucco's restaurant in *The Sopranos*, was on Bloomfield Avenue—at least, until Tony had it firebombed so Uncle Junior couldn't use it as a place to whack Little Pussy.

The Gulch forms the spine of the TV series, too. The famous opening credits sequence follows Tony in his SUV as he leaves the Lincoln Tunnel, passes through Newark (with its water towers painted like buckets), crosses the rusting steel truss bridges that embroider its edges, and then drives up Bloomfield Avenue to the Caldwells. Along the way we glimpse the shotgun step-back houses, sturdy bungalows, the Pizza Land shack, and finally the sweeping lawns of "the heights" (the hilly reaches of central Jersey) where the Soprano family manse sits on its cul-de-sac.

James Gandolfini's parents came at the height of the prewar Italian wave, but moved in a different direction, almost straight north from Newark, at a right angle to the main postwar migration route.

James Joseph Gandolfini was born in Borgo Val di Taro in 1921, on a hillside a little more than a hundred miles outside of Milan, but he moved to the United States as a young man. The Gandolfinis still own land near Milan, a rocky plot the actor would later describe as "mostly covered with snakes." During World War II, the older Gandolfini fought for the American army, winning a Purple Heart. He returned after the war to the area around Paterson and its suburb to the north, Paramus, where he worked as a bricklayer and cement mixer. He worked on the Empire State Building and the George Washington Bridge across the Hudson as a youngster, then worked construction in Jersey until he took the job as head custodian of the Paramus Catholic High School.

His wife, Santa, was born in New Jersey in 1924, but moved back to Naples as a child. She went back and forth her whole life. James and Santa had two daughters, Johanna (now Antonacci), who manages the Family Division of the

Superior Court in Hackensack, and Leta Gandolfini, who would become the chief executive officer of a small dressmaking firm, Sunrise Brands. Johanna is thirteen years older and Leta is eleven years older than James John Gandolfini, the baby of the family. Jamie, as he was known until high school, was born even farther north, in Westwood, New Jersey, on September 18, 1961.

In a family that seemed full of women all old enough (well, to a toddler, anyway) to be his mother, Jamie was the center of everybody's attention. And he learned early how to make all that attention worthwhile. Jamie's cousin, Patricia Gandolfini, remembers one Sunday afternoon when her father, Aldo Gandolfini, had invited his brother James and his family over to Patricia's house in Waldwick to play poker. "I had just gotten my license and wanted to drive everyone everywhere," Patricia wrote in an e-mail exchange with the Bergen County *Record*. So she drove Jamie to the duck pond in Ridgewood, where they bought ice cream and walked around the water. "My mother says when I came home I said to her, 'You know, Jamie was more entertaining than any of the guys I know.' He was always fun, smart, always putting on a show."

When Jamie was beginning grade school, the family decamped to Park Ridge, a suburb planted on the farthest northern border of the state, almost in New York. Park Ridge is only twenty miles from Times Square, but it can seem like it's in a different country—a small, leafy community of around eight thousand, living mostly in Cape Cods, colonials, and ranch houses built in the sixties and seventies around a tiny nineteenth-century core. The downtown is festooned with gingerbread, and the meandering eighteenth- and nineteenth–century roads give it a bucolic charm very different from tract housing suburbs. In the 1970s, it was mostly a blue-collar town.

Don Ruschman, a former mayor of Park Ridge, first noticed Jamie Gandolfini sometime in the seventies, when he started crossing over into Ruschman's backyard from his own in order to play with his daughter. The Gandolfini home on Park Avenue has been razed and replaced with a much larger house built in the past fifteen years or so, but there's a small Cape Cod next door that neighbors remember as all but identical to Jim's first house. The lot, with a big sweep of front yard, is on the town's main street, just a couple of blocks from the town center and Park Ridge High.

"He was a tall, good-looking kid. My daughter knew him better than me, of course, but he was always respectful, kind of quiet," Ruschman says. "I met him later, when he'd return for the local OctoberWoman Foundation for Breast Cancer Research fund-raiser in town every year. When *The Sopranos* was at its height, and people were crazy for it, he was still just a direct, down-to-earth person, totally indifferent to celebrity and all that. Even though he was the biggest draw at every dinner.

"I credit his parents with who he became," Ruschman says. "They were hardworking people who raised their kids and that's who they lived for."

Most of the citizens of Park Ridge in the 1970s were Irish, German, or Italian, and many were Catholic. The town has its own power company and water company, and its own school district, too. High schools all around Park Ridge have graduating classes in the three- to four-hundred-person range, but Park Ridge High School graduates less than a third of those numbers. Thirty years ago the middle school was in the same building as the high school, so kids barely recognized their generational differences—everybody was similar, facing similar prospects, fellow students told me again and again. They were almost like one family.

"We didn't have extremes of poverty or wealth," Ruschman recalls. "Most people were working people, blue-collar people, in those days. Everybody got along. They still do. This sounds like boilerplate, but it's just a great place to raise kids."

Park Ridge is a town built by the American middle class during the era of its greatest security, based on well-paid union jobs and the great economic expansion of the postwar era. Homes sold for $15,000 to $35,000 back in the day; now, when people buy them, at an average price of around $435,000, they sometimes tear down the original and build a McMansion in its place. There's even a new section of town, called the Bear's Nest, with town-houses at $1 million to $1.3 million apiece.

But those are symptoms of a different, more unequal America—the Park Ridge James Gandolfini remembered all his life was a smaller town, almost a village.

"I think I feel a lot," Gandolfini once said, trying to explain how his working-class hometown inflected his whole career. "I never wanted to do business or anything. People interest me, and the way things affect them. And I also have a big healthy affinity for the middle class and the blue collar, and I don't like the way they're treated, and I don't like the way the government is treating them now. I have a good healthy dose of anger about all of that. And I think that if I kept it in, it wouldn't have been very good. I would have been fired a lot. So I found this silly way of living that allows me to occasionally stand up for them a little bit. And mostly make some good money and act like a silly fool."

James and Santa Gandolfini spoke Italian in the home to each other, but not to Jamie and his sisters. Jamie said he could always tell when "they were mad at me in Italian," but even though he traveled back to Italy several times as he grew up, to meet family, he never picked up the language. Assimilation wasn't a choice, it was simply part of growing up. His dad cutting the lawn with a push-mower to the sound of Italian singers on the stereo was about as far as his cultural memory went toward the immigrant experience.

"There were things I did that drove my father nuts, I know," he told Stephen Whitty of *The Star-Ledger* in 2012. "Lying on the couch and then getting up, and thirty-five cents would have fallen out of my pocket and just be lying there on the cushions. Drove him crazy. He said it showed I had no respect for money. Maybe I didn't. Maybe I still don't."

Jamie's father's job at Paramus Catholic pulled long hours but was usually regular and predictable. He'd often have Jamie help out with painting jobs or other mainte-nance work at the school. Jamie's mother worked as a high school lunch lady, first at the Immaculate Heart Academy in Washington Township, and then as cafeteria chief at the nearby Academy of the Holy Angels in Demarest, to make ends meet.

They were people who worked hard, who got up every day and did what had to be done. But in those days you could make a living that way. They bought a little two-family cottage in Lavallette, on the Jersey Shore, renting one side to friends or relatives every summer. After he was fourteen or so, Jamie had a boat at the Shore, a wooden boat with a motor, and he'd go fishing and crab-bing along the coast. Sometimes with a friend, but often alone.

Jamie wasn't entirely sure what he'd inherited from his mother. "I don't know—introspective, depressed, a little judgmental, kind of smart about people," he once said. But thinking about her made him take measure of just how assimilated he thought he really was. Asked, in the middle of *The Sopranos*, what was most Italian about him, Gandolfini said, "Loyalty to friends and family, I think. I guess you'd have to ask them. Stubbornness. I don't know. I think I'm very Italian. I communicate a little bit through yelling. A lot of our family does that. I've been working on that."

Park Ridge High is an imposing three-story brick pile with a six-columned Georgian portico, the flagship of a K through 12 school system that celebrated its two-hundredth anniversary in 2008. For years kids have gathered after school in a frame building right next door that was called Pop's Sweet Shoppe—honestly—for decades (today it's called Marc's Pizzeria, but it's still full of high school kids every afternoon). There's an Astroturfed football field and handsome baseball diamonds just below the old mill race pond behind the fire department, and the whole town is scored by deep-sided creeks shadowed by oaks and maples and lined with cornflowers.

If growing up in Park Ridge in the 1970s sounds less like *The Godfather: Part II* than *Happy Days*, well, brace yourself. Jamie Gandolfini wasn't the Fonz, either. He was more like Richie Cunningham, with a black helmet of hair everyone remembers as "David Cassidy perfect."

"He was a tall, skinny but broad-shouldered guy, he joked around a lot with the girls, teasing them," Julie Luce (née Francke) told me shortly after Gandolfini died. "He played football and basketball, and was well liked by everybody. He was just a fun, fun-loving guy."

Julie had an off-and-on flirtation with Jamie, "like middle school love," she said. "It started petering out in high school. He went off to college and I really didn't see him again." But she doesn't remember him ever being serious about a girl. *Girls* maybe he was serious about, but not *a* girl. He never stuck with one girl through a whole year. Gandolfini would be voted "Best Looking" and "Biggest Flirt" in his senior year, and those jokey titles really seem to have been pretty well accepted, at least in retrospect. Whatever his appeal was to girls in those days, it was "nothing like the appeal he had on *The Sopranos*," Luce says. "That was a role he was playing. It was completely out of character for the guy we knew in school."

Jamie became "Jimmy" by his sophomore year, then "Jim," but by senior year he was "Fini"—pronounced "Feeney," as if he'd assimilated all the way to Irishness. There's an unwritten rule about high school nicknames to the effect that the more generally they're used, the more of a character that person is. By the end of senior year, almost everyone called him Fini.

The teachers who knew Gandolfini say he was never trouble in the classroom, never a discipline problem, but nevertheless a cutup with his tight group of friends. They were "their own best audience," and competed all day long trying to make one another crack up, according to drama teacher Ann Comarato.

Donna Mancinelli was student director in the theater program at Park Ridge, and she decided, with Comarato, to cast Jim in his first speaking role, in *Arsenic and Old Lace,* his junior year. His audition seemed to come out of nowhere. "We were so surprised because he was, like, a jock," Mancinelli recalls.

Somehow, no one knew he was already a triple threat, having participated in theatrical productions all through grade school. He played Dick Deadeye in a third-grade production of *H.M.S. Pinafore.* He was in the school marching band, sang in the choir, and he'd danced a small part in *Can-Can* the year before.

"He was a complete natural on stage right away," Comarato says. "We thought, 'Where have you been all this time?'"

Mostly, he was on the field—freshman year, Gandolfini played baseball, football, and basketball for Park Ridge, and ran some track and field. He could do all those things and, in his junior year, take a part in the seasonal school plays because Park Ridge was so small—a regional high school would have been both more competitive and more specializing. The 165 kids in Gandolfini's class made up one of the largest in the school's history, but it's a lot smaller than those at the other high schools, both public and parochial, nearby in Bergen County. Park Ridge shrunk to as few as forty or so graduates a few years ago, before bouncing back to last year's class of ninety.

Still, Gandolfini had a pretty demanding schedule. He dropped baseball first, after freshman year. Then football; basketball was Gandolfini's best sport, anyway. "He was an all-round athlete, but not really a standout," says Tom Bauer, who was assistant coach of the football team and taught Gandolfini Spanish ("a solid B student," Bauer says). "But at Park Ridge he could play, and do well."

The way theater worked was a drama in the fall and a musical in the spring. There's a pretty little proscenium stage built into the corner of the school building, with a side door that opens a short hop from where Pop's Sweet Shoppe used to be (the state just helped pay for a renovation that painted over the backstage cast graffiti from Fini's years). Although there's a petition going around Park Ridge to name a street after Gandolfini, former mayor Ruschman is trying to get them to name the high school theater for him instead.

In his senior year Fini tried out for the lead in *Kiss Me, Kate,* the Cole Porter hit about a company mounting a musical version of William Shakespeare's *The Taming of the Shrew.* The plot is a complicated confection of backstage romances, but the underlying themes of male vanity and violence winning female sympathy and support are roughly similar.

In Porter's version the final eponymous song is almost a kinky demand to be abused, a "hurt me but don't desert me" number that is meant to show both swagger and real vulnerability. Petruchio, the Shakespeare character, is decked out in a silly Renaissance outfit full of feathers and clashing stripes that's deliberately comical, yet in that ridiculous getup he gives his most heartfelt and abject declaration of love—and wins the shrew.

Both Comarato and Mancinelli thought Gandolfini was perfect for the role. He shared it with another student, part of Park Ridge's everybody-plays ethos, but Fini had the prestigious closing-night performance. Yet, to everyone's dismay, he was having trouble with his first major memorization challenge. During rehearsals he'd shout "Fuck!" when he forgot a line or fumbled a cue, sometimes hitting himself in the head.

"I used to really get on him for that," says Comarato. (Later, after *The Sopranos* became a hit and Gandolfini met Comarato at one of the OctoberWoman fund-raising dinners, he'd send her a note asking her to count how many times he said "fuck" on the air. "And they're paying me for it!" he wrote.) "But it got so bad some of his friends in the play were worried he wouldn't be able to perform."

Sally Zelikovsky played Kate—she was Buttercup in that third-grade *Pinafore*—and she wrote about it on her blog. Zelikovsky lives in California now, where she writes a community blog and is involved with the Tea Party.

"Two weeks before opening night for *Kate*, Jimmy, yes, Emmy award–winning James Gandolfini, did not have his lines or songs memorized," Zelikovsky wrote in a memorial to her classmate a week after his death. "We had been covering for him by ad-libbing cues in anticipation of his lines. With two weeks to go, the musical director threatened to call off the production."

Gandolfini's closest friends in the cast were furious with him. Zelikovsky remembered him responding to the pressure, coming into rehearsal the next day with all his lines memorized. And the performance went very well—just a hint of Fini's future struggles with memorization. Still, nobody thought they had a great actor in their midst.

"Jimmy, surprisingly, pursued it as a career—surprisingly—because if you had taken a senior class survey of the 'most likely to pursue a career in acting,' I don't think Jimmy would have won," Zelikovsky remembered. There were other talents in Park Ridge who seemed much more likely to succeed in the theater, like Karen Duffy, who would achieve a certain fame as a VJ on MTV in the late 1980s (and just happened to move into the same building as Fini in the West Village). Whatever Jim had on stage, it didn't seem theatrical so much as real. Some people remember Gandolfini's star performance as more of a marker of how classless Park Ridge was than as an artist's precocious juvenilia.

Park Ridge High was like any other school, filled with cliques and rivalries, but Zelikovsky thought of them as more "fluid" because it was a small institution. Students couldn't mount a play if they didn't get jocks or burn-outs to help. They couldn't really field a sports team unless artsy students were given a shot.

Placing Gandolfini as a jock or a burn-out or any other binary opposition so popular in high school didn't quite work because so many hats seemed to fit Fini. Had to fit, really.

Much later, after he'd moved to New York City and started taking acting classes, Jim Gandolfini came back to his parents' house in Park Ridge to eat a home-cooked dinner and warn his family that he might be pretty good at this acting thing. If he succeeded as he hoped he would, the attention and publicity might get to be "a pain in the ass." That's when he was considering changing his name to "Jimmy Leather" to spare them the trouble.

At the time, his mom and dad and two sisters laughed at the very idea that Fini would have to change his name to save them from the press hordes that might one day come.

And yet, damn it, they did. Gandolfini said the way things turned out may have "humbled" his sisters a little bit, which was "a good thing."

As Gandolfini's fame grew, especially once *The Sopranos* became a runaway hit, and the reporters did start to come around, James and the family stayed mute. Gandolfini gave very few interviews to the press—you could count the longish ones on one hand—and he insisted on his family's privacy. Friends were asked to avoid the press, too.

Even in 2001, when Donna Mancinelli first got him involved in the OctoberWoman Foundation annual dinners and Tony Soprano was almost as recognizable nationally as Colonel Sanders, he was still insisting on no press. The OctoberWoman Foundation became *The Sopranos'* pet New Jersey charity until the banking crash in 2008 forced the foundation to scale back its fund-raising. Some years, much of the regular cast, from Edie Falco and Michael Imperioli to Tony Sirico and Lorraine Bracco, would appear. The $1,000-a-plate dinners drew as many as a thousand people at their height, and Gandolfini would stand for hours signing autographs and thanking donors. But only HBO cameramen were ever allowed in. TV crews from as far away as Australia were turned down.

Most of the people who knew Gandolfini say he and his sisters are just "very private." Both Leta Gandolfini and Johanna Antonacci declined to be interviewed about their brother; some of his friends also declined, saying Jim had insisted on "almost an *omerta*" when he was alive. And it's true, whenever he could, Gandolfini dodged personal questions.

The people at HBO who worked in publicity for *The Sopranos* or helped manage Gandolfini's career say a celebrity press that often distorts reality out of aimless sensationalism would make anyone reticent. The family has denied the *New York Post*'s account of his last meal, for instance, saying the long list of alcoholic drinks is wrong—the two piña coladas he ordered were actually nonalcoholic drinks for his thirteen-year-old son, and nobody would assign everything on a family bill to one person, anyway. The twenty-four-hour media cycle creates an endless series of factual mistakes and false spins.

The fact that Gandolfini went through a painful divorce right in the middle of *The Sopranos* hoopla in 2002 no doubt encouraged him to batten down the hatches even more. Widely broadcast rumors of drug abuse and wild parties on the set were set off by the presettlement legal jousting, which in turn fed a popular perception that actors *are* the characters they play, especially when they play gangsters.

Some of his Italian-American friends shrug and say Gandolfini was so Italian that reticence with strangers is part of the culture. A man is expected to cut a *bella figura*, dress nicely, show manners in public ("Don't shame the family!"), but draw the drapes at home.

There's that Jersey Jinx to think about, too. The litany of friends and professional colleagues who say James Gandolfini was "a regular Jersey guy" is deafening, so much so that you wonder if he didn't subscribe to some version of that "Nobody from Jersey ever gets credit for nothin'" syndrome. Stick your head up and they'll chop it off. Safer to say you're just like everybody else.

Others say it's more a function of when he achieved success. Coming late to movies, when he was thirty-two, and landing his first lead role, as Tony Soprano, when he was nearing forty, meant that the vast majority of Gandolfini's life was spent outside of the media maelstrom. Young actors often develop a backstory for their offstage persona to help drive interest in their movies, usually one that underlines their stage presence. Jim never had to; by the same token, when he achieved fame, there was no embarrassing "Jimmy Leather" persona to live down, either. You can ask John "Cougar" Mellencamp about what that's like.

"I got successful at a late age, so I'm under no delusions about what all this is about," Gandolfini himself said. "Well, I'm sure I have some delusions. But you know, basically, it's a job. You work hard, and you get tired a little bit, but that's all it is." Being a famous actor was a little like being Geppetto. You work at it and work at it, and one day people may think you've made a real boy. Nothing to fuss over, really.

And there was such a thing as being a good son, too. Nobody fussed over his father's labor or his mother's; whatever Jamie did was all due to them. Success he wanted, of course, most people do, but this sort of monster success, where everyone knows your name and thinks they know *you*—that was embarrassing.

Some of those who knew him the longest say he was always just as shy as he was outgoing, if that makes any sense at all. As a kid, Gandolfini struck some of his friends as particularly gentle and paradoxically solitary. "In sixth grade, when I first met him, what he wanted to be when he grew up was a forest ranger, which seems so kind of low-key and kind of almost quiet and alone," classmate Julie Luce told the Bergen County *Record*. "And I think a little part of that was sort of with him always. He was somebody who did not like the attention. It's, like, contradictory because everyone in the entire planet knew who he was, or most of them did, but he was really very private. . . .

"He was like a really regular person. He tried to live a regular life and I don't know how he did that, but he was able to a little bit, in between the craziness of being a celebrity."

It did seem odd that an actor who was so convincing in the most intimate of performances would just stiff-arm almost all requests for interviews. And it made it very easy for his fans to simply assume he *was* Tony Soprano. People who didn't know him before he got famous slipped and called him "Tony" all the time. After all, he was Italian-American, from Jersey, and he tawked like the Tone. Who else could he be?

And, whatever his reasons were, putting Park Ridge under a kind of media bell jar helped preserve a certain civic pride in appearances. Like a lot of Bergen County, Park Ridge projects an air of being left out of the modern issues roiling America. There are few class conflicts, few ethnic frictions, in Park Ridge. There are also very few African-Americans (one exception was a Park Ridge High School music director, the one who demanded Fini learn his lines or he'd cancel the play). Diversity largely amounts to people with Irish, German, Italian, and Jewish backgrounds. "But we don't think of ourselves that way," Dolly Lewis, a former teacher at Park Ridge High, told me by the town pool one day. "We just think of ourselves as Americans." It's really just a nice place, with strong civic values.

Though, as former mayor Don Ruschman likes to point out, there was that guy who lived in the Gandolfinis' neighborhood, whom everybody knew was a lieutenant in the mob. Not that anybody made a big deal about it. As Ruschman says, chuckling, "He kept his lawn beautifully."

3.

Romantic Lead

After graduation from Park Ridge High in 1979, Gandolfini's mother, Santa, insisted that he go to college. He'd be the first Gandolfini boy to go (both his sisters had attended Rutgers); they thought he should study something useful, like marketing. He didn't want to.

"But then I got there and I thought, jeez, fifty thousand eighteen-year-olds in one place—what the hell was I complaining about?" he said much later. "This is great. I was around a lot of fun people and I had a ball. I had more fun than somebody probably should have and I learned a lot—although I don't think I remember anything from communications."

Gandolfini thrived at Rutgers' flagship campus in New Brunswick, a small former industrial city on the Raritan River. He started to move beyond the quiet, skinny kid he'd been in Park Ridge.

"He told everyone he wanted to be an actor," says Mark Di Ionno, now a columnist and Pulitzer finalist at *The*

Star-Ledger. In the fall of 1979, Di Ionno was a four-year naval veteran who had just doffed his uniform to enroll as a freshman. "Frankly, I didn't recognize his talent at the time. He seemed like just a regular Jersey guy. . . . He was like a lot of us, like I wanted to be a writer. You know, college freshmen in the middle of New Jersey, how the fuck you gonna get there?"

Di Ionno recognized Gandolfini's natural leadership, and that he was often up and down—ebullient, but occasionally moody, like any teenager. Selfish, undisciplined.

But he also saw the beginnings of Gandolfini's first adult crew, the group of guys who would wind up hanging out together all through college and beyond: Jim's roommate, Stewart Lowell, now an accountant for a New York firm, and Di Ionno's roommate, Tony Foster, another Bergen County kid, were among the first. Tom Richardson, who would later work at Gandolfini's production company, Vito Bellino, now an account executive at the *Ledger,* and Mark Ohlstein, a chiropractor, would soon join the group and remain good friends with Gandolfini until his death.

The friendships developed as you might expect, over beer and games; the guys would sometimes engage in a sort of half-comic "fight club" in the halls, whaling on each other. (This is something of a New Jersey tradition—my ten-year-old son did the same thing with his pals in the garage behind our house in South Orange, much to his non-Jersey-born parents' consternation. Everybody seemed to enjoy it tremendously.) Among the inner core of friends, Gandolfini was known as "Buck."

One night, about two or three weeks into freshman year, Di Ionno was awakened by pounding on his door. "Buck got arrested, Buck got arrested!"

Gandolfini had broken one of the wooden traffic barriers that protect the parking lots at Rutgers. "He didn't even have a car," Di Ionno recalls. "The worst thing was that it happened on campus, but somehow he'd been arrested by New Brunswick police, not campus cops.

"I put my uniform back on, because I know they're not going to release him to another student," he continues. "And I go down to the New Brunswick police station and I say, 'I'm here to get James Gandolfini.' So they release him, and I think I wound up going to court with him, too . . . he ended up paying a fine."

The year went on like that. A few months later someone bought a bunch of spring-loaded dart guns—novelty toys that shot little plastic sticks with rubber suction cups on one end—and they started having *High Noon* gun battles throughout the dorm.

After removing the suction cups, of course, so they'd hurt more when you got hit.

"So [Gandolfini] runs into his room, he doesn't see me," Di Ionno says. "I come up behind him, just outside his door, gun in my hand, and I kick it—Bam!—and the metal doorknob smashes right into his face. I had no idea he'd turned back. I open the door and he's knocked out, he's unconscious, blood all over, and I'm like, 'Oh, shit, what did I do?' I thought I fucking killed the kid. I ended up taking him to St. Peter's [hospital]."

Jim got a few stitches, for which Di Ionno paid the $25 fee. But that scar on Gandolfini's forehead, the one that became so expressive on *The Sopranos* when he was angry at another mobster or begging for respite from his wife's impatience? That was a Rutgers dorm gun battle wound.

Di Ionno said Gandolfini always had a kind of mutual loyalty bond with his friends, an understood promise that they'd always be there for each other. Even after freshman year, when many of the guys, including Gandolfini, moved off campus, the group hung together, adding members now and then.

Buck took a job at the campus pub as a bouncer and bartender, at $3.50 an hour. In those days, campus pubs were a much bigger deal than they are today. The Vietnam War had set up the irony that eighteen-year-olds could be drafted and killed or maimed abroad, but could not order a Budweiser at home. So the drinking age was lowered in most states to eighteen in the late 1960s, and four-fifths of the student body qualified. The pubs grew until they seemed to absorb the student centers that had established them. The Rutgers pub would invite musical acts—real acts, not one guy with an acoustic guitar—and major speakers. After the Mothers Against Drunk Driving campaign began in the mid-1980s, states raised the legal drinking age back to twenty-one, and campus pubs shrank back to their larval stage as if they'd eaten magic mushrooms.

But back in 1980 the Rutgers pub was a scene, and Jim Gandolfini seemed to enjoy it enormously. He was, to boot, the kind of strong guy who was amiable enough to defuse any conflict before it got out of hand. He often did front-door ID checking, greeting customers, setting the tone; but he pulled the heavy duty, too, hefting kegs, mopping out, all the drudge work. And, like all good bartenders, he took care of his friends.

That's where he met Tom Richardson, also a bouncer at the pub, who became one of Jim's closest friends and project manager at his film and TV production company, Attaboy Films. Richardson was an Irish guy from West Orange, who had his first taste of mozzarella with tomato and basil leaves plucked from Gandolfini's father's garden behind their little two-family summer place on the Shore, in Lavallette ("*Marone,* where you been all your life, never had tomato, cheese, and basil!"). Richardson's roommate Mark Ohlstein was a regular, too, along with all the dorm crew. It was almost like forging a new, on-site family, which just happened to have the same all-for-one attitudes, and more often than not the same class origins, as the gang of kids in Park Ridge.

"For the last two years at Rutgers, Jimmy drove around campus in this black Ford Falcon he'd gotten, from his father, I think," says a fellow classmate. "He loved that car. Just loved it. In part because it was like a big 'Fuck you!' to the guys at Rutgers who drove around in fancy sports cars."

The 1962 Falcon had been his father's car, kept in mint condition, and giving it to Jim was, for Mr. Gandolfini, a test of the boy's maturity. One that he did not pass with flying colors. One summer Jim drove the whole crew down to the Shore in the Falcon. Just as they picked up one of the guys in front of his parents' house, the engine caught fire. They had to put it out with a fire extinguisher.

"Jim really loved his parents," one of the guys remembers. "Ruining the car's hood like that was just terrible in his dad's eyes. I can remember Jim standing with his dad, hanging his head, as Mr. Gandolfini, who was a lot shorter and slighter than Jim, lectured him over what he'd done to his car. But he never had it repainted or anything. He just drove it around like it was."

Stories about Gandolfini's physical fearlessness often go hand-in-hand with tales about his remarkable strength. Not just carrying kegs at the pub, but standing up to challenges. There'd be fights between students every now and then; and he'd break them up, often genially, but with a sobering display of muscle. A couple of Jim's friends remember two pickup trucks filled with five or six guys squealing their tires in the pub parking lot one night. Jim was just getting off shift, and he went out to tell them off. They surrounded Gandolfini, but he stood his ground until the pub bouncers heard what was happening and scared them off. "He wasn't afraid of anything," a friend recalls.

Sophomore year Gandolfini moved out of the dorms and into the Birchwood Terrace Apartments on Hamilton Street (the building is still there), not far from the Rutgers campus. It became the center of his life for the rest of his years in college. When he graduated in 1983, he'd tell everyone that his degree was in marketing or communications—although his Rutgers transcript actually gives his degree as in "journalism"—but he was quick to say he didn't remember much about marketing.

Maybe the most curious thing about his time at Rutgers is he never tried to go on stage while he was there. He told all his friends he was going to be an actor, but he didn't try out for campus plays. The university, like all major state schools, has an active theater department, with a professional staff, and they mount dramas and musicals every year. But Gandolfini wasn't a theater major, and the Mason Gross School of the Arts at Rutgers restricts roles for its students. The university has no record of Gandolfini appearing in any unaffiliated plays or performances on campus over his full four years.

It's rare for a major talent to simply not seek expression, especially in acting, which has many more ingénues than it does older character actors. Was he unsure of his commitment, or did he doubt he could actually make it as an actor?

Di Ionno remembers one attempt Gandolfini made to

land a theater job, after freshman year. When classes ended, Gandolfini asked Di Ionno if he'd join him on a road trip to North Carolina, where students could try out for summer stock. So the two of them, anticipating all the adventures a road trip could offer, loaded up Di Ionno's car and headed south.

"And he failed. He failed miserably," Di Ionno recalls. "He was just very disappointed in how bad he seemed to be. . . . I remember driving home, he was angry with himself. He felt he'd been unprepared, that he'd given the thing no thought about what he might be asked to do, or something. And he was just very upset that he'd done that."

As far as anyone can tell, he didn't try out for acting again for another five or six years.

Gandolfini did get serious about a girl in those years, for the first time, really. By the summer after his sophomore year he and Lynn Marie Jacobson, whom he'd met as a bouncer at the campus pub when she was a waitress, were close, even though she was a couple of years older. By 1981, when she graduated, she was always at the Birchwood.

Friends remember Lynn as "classically beautiful"—so pretty, in fact, that she intimidated some of Jimmy's buddies. She had auburn hair, dressed more formally than most of the other kids, and was nice, friendly, nothing off-putting about her, but serious, older than most of Jimmy's crew. She was from West Caldwell, and studied advertising. After she graduated, she got a job in New York City at the Media Management Public Relations and Advertising Company during the day, and several nights a week she also worked late hours as a hostess at The Manor, a sort of banquet room–conference center in West Orange.

Lynn worked two jobs to help her family with her tuition costs; she had a twin sister, Leslie Ann, and another sister, Gail, who still lived with her parents. She'd pull long hours a few days a week, doing her day job in the city and then schlepping up to The Manor until closing. The hours were a little unpredictable—these sorts of catered complexes are fairly common in Jersey, and they host events of all sorts, with schedules set by the group or firm that rents the space.

Lynn was driving back to Caldwell on a Sunday morning around 4:45 A.M. when her car crossed Bloomfield Avenue and hit a utility pole. She was almost home—the accident happened right where the road curves to enter Caldwell, just east of 180 Bloomfield Avenue. Lynn's car, a 1971 Ford Mustang, was cut in half, and the front end smashed into a storefront a few feet farther on. She was killed instantly. She was twenty-two years old.

The police found no mechanical problem or anything else in the car to explain the crash. Everyone assumed she'd fallen asleep at the wheel after a very long week.

When you're just nineteen and a tragedy of such adult scale happens, friends are often so shocked they don't know what to do. Especially since it seemed sort of out of character for a guy like Gandolfini to be touched by death. He was still a junior in college, majoring in the same practical subject Lynn had studied. The night after Jim learned about Lynn's accident, just two friends went to his apartment at the Birchwood and let themselves in. Jim was there, drinking wine and watching television. The three spent the night together, now and again smoking marijuana, but mostly just sitting in front of the TV, talking about this and that. Every now and then, for no reason— for every reason—Jimmy would start to cry.

Everyone came to the funeral, of course, at Saint Peter's Episcopal Church in Essex Fells. Jimmy was, several friends told me, "the boyfriend" at the funeral, helping the whole family, but trying in particular to console Lynn's twin sister. The burial was in East Hanover.

In some sense the shock never left him. When he won his third Emmy as lead actor in a drama in 2003, Gandolfini—after blowing a raspberry into the microphone because he'd promised his son, Michael, that he would—said: "I'd like to dedicate this to the memory of a girl I knew a long time ago who basically, inadvert . . . I can't say that word. She made me be an actor. Her name was Lynn Jacobson, and I miss her very much."

It was typical Jim, playing peekaboo with his real life, without really explaining what Jacobson meant to him. People who watched the Emmys that year could be forgiven for assuming she was a favorite drama teacher, or maybe someone who'd convinced him to pursue his true ambitions in life, that sort of typical, celebrity-acceptance-speech sentiment.

"She was a smart, lovely girl who worked two jobs to get her way through college and help her family," Gandolfini told *GQ* correspondent Chris Heath in 2004, in the only interview that ever got Jim to open up about Jacobson. Her sudden death "made me very angry . . . I think I was studying advertising or something before that, and after that I changed a little bit. You know, it must have changed me a little bit.

"If anything, it was 'Why plan for the future? Fuck it.' It was like, 'Fuck this.'"

That's the most he ever said about Lynn in public. According to friends who knew him at the time, he said little more in private. But in his stiff-lipped, understated way, Gandolfini saw her death as a turning point. It left him with something inside he could not express, something that could not be assuaged by roughhousing or parties or, well, anything less than artistic expression.

"Yeah, I think I might not have done what I've done," he told Heath. "I don't know what I'd have done. I think it definitely pushed me in this direction. I don't know why. Just as a way to get out some of those feelings. I don't know."

At the same time that Gandolfini was going through Rutgers, a true revolution in American cooking was moving east from California. As late as the mid-1970s, salad dressing in the United States was, like fried potatoes, usually called "French," and most sauces were just "gravy" (which to most Italian-Americans meant tomato sauce—Jerseyans like Paulie Walnuts still call it that). But on the West Coast there were already fads building for fresh ingredients, traditional recipes, and "artisanal" (as they'd come to be known) cheeses, sausages, coffees, you name it.

More than many students, Gandolfini wanted to earn extra money, but like most, he really wasn't qualified to do much more than tend bar. But by 1982, Gandolfini applied for a job at Ryan's, a new bar/restaurant in New Brunswick that tried to set a higher standard—and promised better tips.

New Brunswick in the early 1980s was still, even near the campus, rather run-down. Customers complained about the street Ryan's was on, about parking in a dingy nabe that had some of them darting to their cars when they left. But they came anyhow. It was a white-tablecloth kind of place, with the start of a decent cellar and an interest in trends that were only then starting to be called "foodie." Gandolfini tended bar there for two years, beginning a pretty serious involvement with nightlife that would be a part of his working life for years.

"We met shortly after Lynn died," says T.J. Foderaro, a wine critic and journalist who back then worked as a waiter at Ryan's. Gandolfini and Foderaro became good friends; five nights a week they spent late nights closing down the restaurant and then wandering out for a night-cap. They'd talk about books, poetry, philosophy. Foderaro says he was in his "serious young man" stage, reading Dostoyevsky and the like, bringing a copy of Allen Ginsberg's "Howl" in to read aloud while the waitstaff cleaned the grill. He presented a copy as a gift to his new friend, who seemed to really get a kick out of it. But Jim also had a blue edge, as T.J. soon discovered.

"He was in the throes of [mourning for Jacobson] for years," T.J. remembers. "Sometimes he'd talk about it—I remember, every now and then, at a party or after everyone had left the restaurant, he'd be sitting there alone, with tears running down his face.

"Occasionally he'd start to talk about her, but the second he felt you might think he was exploiting it, or you tried to console him, that was it."

Foderaro remembers Jim keeping a yellow Labrador retriever at the Birchwood apartment building. Gandolfini had shared him with Lynn when she was alive, and for Jim, the dog seemed to keep her alive, too, somehow.

It wasn't as if her death doomed his chances at love, exactly. Women were always attracted to Jim, T.J. says, and not just because he was tall and good-looking back then.

"He was the most complex and demanding relationship I ever had," Foderaro says. "Because he didn't want to have any kind of superficial relationship. He wanted to talk to you honestly, and when he locked eyes with you he wanted you to connect to him on a very deep level, and he didn't tolerate bullshit. He didn't want you to put up defenses, or pretend to be something you weren't. He wanted to get you, and he wanted you to get him, and he really meant it.

"And girls loved that."

Toward the end of their years at Rutgers Foderaro became the manager at a new restaurant, The Frog and Peach (named for a Peter Cook/Dudley Moore sketch, but also a four-star, white-tablecloth kind of place—it's still open). The chef was another Rutgers guy, an out-of-state student (they pay a much higher tuition) named Mario Batali, whose family had been involved in making and selling Italian cuisine on the West Coast since 1903. The foods his family championed required hand labor—Italian sweet sausages, fresh pastas, hand-dipped cheeses, that sort of thing. The labor made them expensive, but insisting on traditional methods was a mark of quality in a country taken over by food production on an industrial, corporate-run scale.

Foderaro introduced the rotund, red-haired Batali to Gandolfini, and they became good friends, too. The three of them would talk food and wine in the same way T.J. and Jim talked books and philosophy. Later, when Batali became an expert on classical Italian cuisine and a famous chef with restaurants in San Francisco, Los Angeles, and New York, Gandolfini became a regular on both coasts. Rutgers decided to include both Gandolfini and Batali in an award ceremony for distinguished graduates a couple of years ago, and the two old friends trooped on stage relatively abashed. Most of their fellow honorees were scientists and historians, a computer whiz, that kind of thing; Gandolfini, always self-deprecating, would tell the press that he and Batali had followed all these brainiacs to the podium with some trepidation, like "Heckle and Jeckle" bringing up the end.

But Jim really did learn his wines in those years, and a lot about food. It was a foundation for earning a living, of course, but it was also a real education, one earned in good company and with plenty of real experience. Italian-American food in New Jersey is not quite the same thing—actually, *The Sopranos* would devote an episode to the difference, distinguishing between classical cuisine and dishes like "gabagool." We'll come back to this topic later, since it cycles through Gandolfini's life at every stage, but it's important to understand that it's a more serious issue than the actor himself ever acknowledged in public.

Foderaro hired another student, Roger Bart, a senior at Mason Gross School of the Arts, to act as bartender at The Frog and Peach. Late each evening Gandolfini would drop by to help close the place, drinking wine for free and schmoozing with the staff, before wandering off into the night with T.J. Maybe because he was tending bar himself at Ryan's, Jim gravitated to Bart, and they struck up a friendship.

"I grew fond of Jim right away," Bart recalls. "He was an affable guy, you could see how he might be a bartender.

But he had this way of looking down when he talked to you—there was this vein of sadness in him."

Bart found Gandolfini's presence striking, but kind of hard to place. "He was also very smart, he and T.J. would have very intellectual conversations, they were both very well read, even though he had this Jersey working-class image going, too," Bart says. "And he was just very sharp, he had a really sharp sense of humor. . . . I'm a pretty funny guy, but Jimmy was always right there with it. And I think I could tell there was this volcanic temper just underneath. . . . Oh, yeah, you could see that, even then."

Bart asked Gandolfini if he'd ever thought of acting, and he replied, "No," pretty gruffly, as if that were somehow out of the question. Bart had spent the past three years learning the stage at Mason Gross, and he was consumed with worry about how he would ever find his footing as an actor when he graduated. There seemed to be a huge gulf between doing a school play and building a career.

"You've got to remember, I was twenty-one, twenty-two; most of what I talked to Jimmy about was type," Bart recalls. "You know, stereotype? At that age, you're wondering what you can play, what sort of part you can get, that might add up to a living. Being cast in a conservatory school like Mason Gross is such an easy thing, you ask a guy you know or sometimes you just read your name on a list. But out in the real world, how do you get on stage?

"I was like, a hundred and thirty pounds, with this voice that gets so high," Bart says, demonstrating. "So I was kind of mystified about how to make it myself. But I could see Jimmy's type right off. He was tall, six-one or six-two, obviously just really strong physically. And he was a real Jersey guy, but I kept thinking to myself that New Jersey could use its own Gene Hackman. So I told him so, and I think some of the comparisons I made maybe resonated with movies he'd liked and things he'd admired. It wasn't like I was telling him, 'Oooh, you could be in commercials!'"

Bart thought in particular about a teacher he had at Rutgers, Kathryn Gately, and the patient way she'd worked with a big slab of an Irish guy who Bart thought hadn't half the spark Gandolfini did. She'd been patient and supportive, using the Sanford Meisner method to promote immediacy and bring out a deep-buried forcefulness in his performance. Bart could imagine her working with Jim and finding it much more rewarding.

So he kept mentioning it to Gandolfini, whenever they were together socially. Jim would tell him, "Yeah, I mean to, I should," but he never did. Bart didn't give up.

Then a funny thing happened. Six weeks after he graduated from Rutgers and had found himself an apartment in Jersey City, Bart got called back for the part of Tom Sawyer in Broadway's *Big River*, a musical adaptation of Mark Twain. He had a career in show business.

Still, the Rutgers crew would get together every now

and then, in Jersey and in Manhattan, where a lot of them drifted soon after school. Whenever Bart saw Jimmy, he'd recommend Kathryn Gately. Bart wasn't sure why Gandolfini didn't just call her, but he never dropped it. It wasn't personal, it was just business.

When Gandolfini graduated in 1983, he took an apartment for about a year with his former roommate, Stewart Lowell, in Hoboken. The whole neighborhood all around was undergoing a big renewal, but their apartment was not—it was a tiny tenement hutch carved out of a bigger space to rent to people who couldn't afford Manhattan.

It was on the fourth floor. It was very small—two bedrooms, but with only a half wall between them—and hot as an oven in the summer. Anybody who thinks the top floor in a northeastern city tenement has to be the hottest because its roof is exposed to the sun all day just doesn't understand five-floor walk-up physics. It's hotter in the middle, where the air circulates like mud. Air-conditioning would have been an extravagance, and anyway they'd have to lug the machine up four flights, as they'd just done with their refrigerator. The boys bought fans and left them on all the time instead. They helped drown out the noises from the building, too.

Lowell's first job was at McCann-Erickson, the advertising firm, so he commuted to Manhattan every day. Soon Jim had landed a bartending gig at an expensive wine bar on the Upper East Side, where he could walk away each night with $100 to $125 in tips, very sweet in those days. He did odd jobs, too, worked construction, filled in as a bouncer now and then.

"He was a survivor," a friend who knew him in those days says. "He always had a job. He was never lazy, always pitched in, and somehow, whenever he got a job, he'd always be right up there with the owner, or anyway with the most important people."

One day, Gandolfini answered a newspaper ad and was offered the chance to manage a pricey New York nightclub.

It was called Private Eyes, on West Twenty-first Street, in the trendy club district in those days, and it was one of the first video clubs in Manhattan. Every wall was lined with rows of TV sets held by steel and aluminum racks, and they'd play music and art videos all night long. Madonna arranged advanced screenings of videos at Private Eyes; Andy Warhol would show every now and then; at one party an eight-year-old Drew Barrymore was underfoot. Sleek and techno, Private Eyes was large, though nothing like the nearby four-level Area club of the same era. It was the time when video killed the radio star, and Private Eyes took the winner's side.

Private Eyes wasn't cheap—a beer could go for $20, very stiff in those days—and it catered to a wealthy, Long Island clientele. It was a diverse eighties crowd. Gandolfini himself later described the club as being "gay two nights of the week, straight two nights, and then everybody for the last two nights." The club did downtown mini social events, like hosting the debut of a play for video by *The Village Voice* gossip columnist Michael Musto, that kind of thing.

It was a big job. Gandolfini remembered he might have ordered a whole year's supply of liquor in his first week, with nowhere to put it all. Still, the owner, Robert Shalom, had faith in the big twenty-two-year-old Gandolfini.

"I've been thinking back to those days, and the fact that he got this job when he was that young to run Private Eyes, which was a pretty big nightclub, shows something about him," Foderaro says. "I mean, I was just hanging out there with him. But he was managing a really hip, big-deal club, a whole team of bouncers, waitstaff, buying the beer, wine, everything—it was a real job."

Gandolfini had been a bouncer at clubs before, and he was obviously the sort of staffer entertainment venues like to have around. Several friends said he "enjoyed" bouncing, because finding the psychological insight that gave you an edge against anyone, no matter how drunk or how big, was fascinating.

He moved to Manhattan for good, though without taking an apartment of his own. He was making good money at the club, but not that good—and he had better uses for the money he made than paying a mortgage. Managing a club also meant (within reason) being the one person who had to stay sober. It meant assessing a situation quickly, and taking responsibility when things happen that are in no way predictable.

Running a place like Private Eyes showed you a lot of life, exposed you to people from all over and the vices they indulged in. It's not quite stand-up comedy, and it isn't community policing, either, or even the emergency medical service—but it definitely means you versus a crowd, every night.

"The thing about Jim was he was just fantastically strong, and fearless," remembers Foderaro. "I remember one time we went to a convenience store in downtown Manhattan after the club had closed, this was like two A.M., and there were some black guys outside the store who started taunting us. And Jim gave right back. . . . He sort of focused on this one dude, and they started really dishing it back and forth. And Jim, he loved this, you could tell he was really into it.

"We go into the store and they follow us, so it goes on inside the store, and you could see right away the store owner is not real keen on this," Foderaro continues. "And all of a sudden Jim goes right up to this one guy who was taunting us, like really nose-to-nose. And he came at this guy, who was bigger than Jim, with such force and determination that he basically just backed out of the store and ran away. Jim projected this monster energy."

The gig at Private Eyes lasted a year or so. Gandolfini could have gone on, taken another nightclub job maybe, but he told friends he didn't want to. He went back to construction and odd jobs for a while. He did a little indoor renovation, he even sold books on the street. He seemed unusually proud of his construction labor. Once, in 2002, he offered to drive a writer home after an interview, one of those spontaneous acts of kindness he seemed prone to take, and as the reporter hopped out Gandolfini leaned over to the passenger's side and looked fondly up at the building. He recognized it—he "did a little carpentry here" in the old days.

Roger Bart remembers some kind of job at Astor Place Liquors, on the edge of the NYU campus. He'd see Jimmy lugging mixed boxes of fine wines on the sidewalk—Bart thinks somehow the owner or the staff were friends of Jim's—and they'd talk. Bart would remind him about Kathryn Gately, who had left Rutgers and was running a conservatory at the Nat Horne Studios in Manhattan (the forerunner of the Gately Poole Conservatory she runs today in Chicago).

Gandolfini was now twenty-five. He seemed "wide-eyed" at the prospect, but still, Bart had to call Gately and plead for him. She was running an advanced class. Gandolfini hadn't been on stage since he washed out at summer stock tryouts in 1980. Could she at least see Gandolfini, to take measure of what Roger saw in him? Bart arranged for his friend to call the teacher in her office.

"And then he asked what no other student before or since has ever asked," remembers Gately. "He said he wanted to do the interview, but he wanted to do it over a good meal. So I trooped uptown to this restaurant that had white tablecloths and met this well-dressed young man, so tall, towering, I thought. And he conducted that interview. And the food was great. It really was. . . . It was like a presentation, he told me about everything, it was so Italian. He seemed to have so much dignity. And of course, he was accepted."

4.

Learning How to Act

Once in Gately's class, Gandolfini reacted as he often would—with self-doubt. He wondered almost immediately if he was in over his head.

"When he came to me he wanted to play your average suburban nice guy, the leading-man type," Gately says. "I don't know how to say this—it was like he wanted to be Troy Donahue. And I of course could see that he could be much more than that."

Learning you're not Troy Donahue is not, perhaps, the worst news a serious young actor can hear. But learning that, for stage purposes, you are *not you* is an essential step toward becoming an actor. As Roger Bart had been trying to tell Gandolfini ever since Rutgers, it's the strange synergy between an actor and a part that makes a career. What Bart saw in Gandolfini was an ability to play against his intimidating heavy stereotype. And to make that work, he'd need training.

Gately's reputation was based on teaching the Meisner

technique, a variant on method acting developed by San-ford Meisner after he had worked with Stella Adler and Lee Strasberg at the Group Theatre in New York in the 1940s. It evolved, ultimately, from the Stanislavski system. Meisner became one of the first teachers at The Actors Studio in New York when it was founded, in 1947, by Elia Kazan and Robert Lewis. The technique was first devel-oped for the stage, but like all method acting, its greatest impact has been on film acting.

Meisner technique begins with a series of exercises that are used to heighten observation and influence actor re-sponses through repetition. Two actors will stand in front of the class and begin a dialogue by repeating each other's comments—"You're nervous," for example, followed by "I'm nervous?" "Yes, you're nervous," and so on, in order to elicit spontaneity from the actors. The exercises build over time until they generate enough natural interaction to support a dramatic text.

One of the first exercises Gandolfini encountered was "threading the needle"—literally, threading a needle in front of the class. It looked a little nuts, but he also thought it was like a challenge, a dare: Could he do something like that? "I was immediately interested and scared to death," Gandolfini told Beverly Reid of *The Star-Ledger*. "It really made me very nervous—and I was shocked by that, really. So I ended up staying two years."

"He brought just the tiniest needle with the tiniest eye you can imagine," Gately says, "and he couldn't do it to save his life." If you think that should be easy, try it in front of a group of observant strangers. The idea is for an actor to develop an ease on stage or before the camera that make it appear as if he or she is acting as naturally and confidently as they would in real life.

That sounds all nice and dry and practical, but actors—often the ones who quit the technique—describe the training as difficult and even psychologically invasive.

The best joke about method acting ever told came from Laurence Olivier, on the set of *Marathon Man,* as he waited to do a key confrontation scene with Dustin Hoffman. Hoffman had just been running around a track to recreate the situation of his character, who had been pursued through the city only to wind up, sweaty and disheveled, at the mercy of Olivier's Nazi dentist. As Hoffman sat, huffing and puffing, waiting for cameras to roll, Olivier is reported to have said, "My dear boy, have you ever tried *acting*?"

Studying the Meisner system, its practitioners say, isn't like that anymore, if it ever was; those stories about retrieving buried memories to evoke real emotions, or living like a blind man for a month to play King Lear, are all exaggerated. They are remnants of the 1950s fad for shamanlike authenticity in artistic expression. There are tricks any actor uses—as Gandolfini himself said, staying up all night the night before, or putting a sharp rock in your shoe, will help you simulate anger. What contemporary method actors do have in common is not so much a set of techniques but a conviction that acting has a serious purpose. To do it well you must prepare your mind to convey emotion clearly and immediately. And doing that requires a certain amount of individual psychological integrity, even fearlessness.

Teaching involved a series of exercises designed to make an actor function in the moment, with lightning-quick responses. Much of the work was deeply psychological—not in an analytical way, but in the sense of finding deep emotions that could, with discipline, be applied to a character on stage or camera. Students were supposed to come in with situations and props that would help them bring out such emotional authenticity. Sometimes a teacher or a student would do something to the actor or to his props to provoke a reaction, and that could, given the tensions in the classroom, unleash unpredictable emotion. That usually accounted for the "psychologically invasive" charge.

Gately remembers Gandolfini having particular trouble with crying. "His class was full of women, far outnumbering the men, and they of course could cry very convincingly," she says. Their ease intimidated Jim. "He'd say, 'I want to cry like Melanie,' and I'd tell him he could cry, but it would be different. . . .

"There was another man, John Hall, in the class, he was big too, six-two or six-three, who had the same problem, and they came to me together to ask for a special class," Gately says. "So I did it with them. I think it took three hours, and the only way it would work was when they regressed to childhood."

Gately describes a hilarious scene with two hulking wannabe actors lying on cots in the studio, struggling to regress to a point where tears would flow, each quietly observing the other while Gately coached them in turn. She could feel the competitive tension, but a breakthrough seemed elusive.

Finally a way opened up. For Gandolfini, tears were a function of helplessness. He could make them come only when he imagined himself tied to a chair, with something relentlessly bearing down upon him—"Otherwise, I'd *do* something," he told Gately.

While that kind of personal insight was not the main object of the classes, such unexpected truths were often a by-product of the technique. It was a two-way street. Gately told Jim a personal story about her father: When she was a girl in Boston, her dad would often have Jesuit priests over for disputation (Gately was raised Irish Catholic, but her father was a skeptic), and she was always allowed to sit in on the arguments. They were cheerful dinners, full of declarative summations and their ripostes.

When her father died, for some reason Gately couldn't cry throughout the family services. When finally she went up to his casket, she saw the ring on her father's hand, and somehow it reminded her of those Jesuit dinners, to which she had always been welcome, even as a girl. And suddenly the tears flowed. She was surprised that such a small token could provoke such a profound reaction in her. That was the sort of memory that could serve you on camera.

Gandolfini listened intently, Gately recalls, to that story.

Training at the Gately Poole Conservatory took two years, in two nine-month sessions. The first session was devoted to developing the various tools of the technique, the second to prepping an actual text. Many of the students actually had Broadway parts already, and were making their way toward careers. Gandolfini had no real acting credits but he threw himself into the process. "He was very competitive," Gately says. "If he saw good work, he'd either be depressed, thinking he couldn't match it, or he'd be inspired to work even harder, try to equal it."

It was toward the end of the first session when Gandolfini had the breakthrough he described on *Inside the Actors Studio,* earning the advice he said meant so much to him: "This is what people pay for. . . . They don't wanna see the guy next door."

"The scene," Gately explains, "was about a man learning his wife had been unfaithful, and how he reacts. And Jim came in with all these ideas about backstory, all these little props that made his character, in his imagination. But he was doing it as appearance—he was acting as he thought an actor should to present such a character. Not stiff-lipped, exactly, but very controlled in his actions, very, well, Troy Donahue."

They did the scene four times, on the last night before

the long weekend, and Gandolfini and his acting partner were both deeply frustrated. So was Gately. In fact, so was the whole class.

"I could tell he was very mad at me," Gately said. "He couldn't understand what I wanted. And we were so tired of the scene, we all were. But I said we'd come back to it the next week, and finally get it right, and you could hear groans. . . ."

And, just as his Park Ridge High School friends had jumped in to make sure Gandolfini memorized his lines for *Kiss Me, Kate,* the class took a hand.

"I believe they got together over the weekend and worked on it more," Gately recalls. "And when they came in that [next] week, you could tell they'd put a great deal of work into it. I suggested the actor who was in the scene with Jim should interrupt him or talk over him in some way. And then, wow!"

"I think [the acting teacher] told a partner to do something to me," is how Gandolfini remembered the moment. "And he did it, and I destroyed the place. Y'know, just all that crap they have on stage. And then she said, at the end of it—I remember my hands were bleeding a little bit and stuff, and the guy had left—and she said, 'See? Everybody's fine. Nobody's hurt. This is what you have to do. This is what people pay for. . . . They don't wanna see the guy next door. These are the things you need to be able to express, and control, work on the controlling part, and that's what you need to show.'"

Susan Aston came to New York City just as James Gandolfini was leaving school to find real acting jobs anywhere he could. It was April 1987. She had a paying job in a play and an apartment waiting for her—she was already a member of the Screen Actors Guild, for her small part in *Tender Mercies*, Oscar-winner Robert Duvall's picture about a country music singer's come-from-behind comeback. Her father had worked for the air force when she was growing up, everywhere from Guam to back in the States, but to her, Abilene, Texas, where she lived the longest and went to high school, was home.

Aston has cornflower-blue eyes and a mop of strawberry-blond hair, and the Lone Star twang has never entirely left her voice. She was raised Church of Christ, a Christian sect that thinks the Southern Baptists trend toward sophistication and backsliding. But she loved acting, and being in a play in New York was something she'd always wanted to do.

But plays close, as hers did, and she found out that her apartment, which someone in the theater had arranged for her, was an illegal sublet and she had to leave. She spent a few months sleeping on friends' floors; she slept on a futon behind a row of filing cabinets for a while. Then a friend asked her to help find an actor for a one-act play, *Big El's Best Friend,* about a woman in love with Elvis Presley and an Elvis impersonator. She went around to a cattle-call audition for another play in search of an Elvis.

There on stage was a six-foot-tall skinny guy with slicked-back black hair and a booming nasal voice. The accent was New Jersey, but the honking sound penetrated. Everybody at the audition thought he was completely wrong for the part they were casting, so Aston introduced herself to James Gandolfini and asked if he'd like to impersonate Elvis.

Big El's Best Friend became Gandolfini's first appearance on a New York stage. Aston got cast, too, as a friend of the Elvis fan who was herself slightly smitten. Aston says his southern accent wasn't key to the part, he just imitated the King's slurred Memphis drawl and the way it could turn whole sentences into a single word. According to a memoir by actress Melissa Gilbert, who played the Elvis-loving lead, *Big El's Best Friend* was part of a night of one-acts in which everybody got black eyes: an actor in one of the other plays walked into an open cupboard, Gilbert's boyfriend elbowed her in the eye in his sleep just before opening night, and at some point Aston and Gandolfini got into a stage fight and accidentally gave each other shiners, one apiece.

The play got some notice on the Lower East Side, where it was performed on a basement stage—Elvis, really the cheesy Pop Elvis of painted plaster busts and sequined jumpsuits, was an iconic figure for hip downtowners in those days. *Big El* wasn't a breakout hit by any means. But it did make an acting team out of Aston and Gandolfini, one that would endure, with gaps here and there, until his death.

Back then, Aston and Gandolfini were Gotham out-siders together. He didn't have a place to stay, either, and bridge-and-tunnel people were tolerated by Manhattanites in ways similar to the forbearance shown Southerners. In 1988, T. J. Foderaro's sister Lisa Foderaro, then an enter-tainment writer for *The New York Times*, wrote a feature about young people trying to move to the city as rent-stabilized apartment rules began to evaporate and prices soared. Illegal sublets were the norm, with all their unpre-dictability, but preferable to being on the hook for $1,500 a month for a legal space the size of your mother's sewing room back home. The story cited a struggling actor's un-usual achievement of living in the city for four years with-out ever putting his name on a lease.

Then there is Jim Gandolfini, who seems to thrive on the apartment-hopping life. Since moving to New York City four years ago, Mr. Gandolfini, 26 years old, has never had his name on a lease, never paid more than $400 a month in rent and never lived in one place more than 10 months. His wanderer's existence has given him sojourns, some as brief as two months, in Hoboken, N.J.; Astoria, Queens; Clinton and the Upper West Side of Manhattan, and Park Slope and Flatbush in Brooklyn.

"Moving, to me, is no big deal," said Mr. Gandolfini, whose calling is the theater but whose living comes mostly from bartending and construction. "I have a system down. I throw everything in plastic garbage bags and can be situated in my new place in minutes. Without my name on a lease, I'm in and out. I have no responsibilities."

That was Gandolfini's first mention in *The Times*.

For the next two and a half years Gandolfini and Aston would develop a showcase titled *Tarantulas Dancing*, first as a one-act, then with a second act added. They performed at all sorts of stages around the city, from the Samuel Beckett Theatre on Theatre Row to the basement stage at the West Bank Café on Forty-second Street, which was managed in those days by Yale theater grad Lewis Black (who later became famous for his splenetic rants on *The Daily Show*). Directed by Aston and written by a friend specifically for the two of them, *Tarantulas Dancing* takes place as Aston's character, called "M'Darlin'," has decided to break it off with Gandolfini, who's named "Bucky." The MacGuffin is an electric steam iron Bucky claims as his and wants back.

It's a play about opposites attracting one another, and a kind of duel between their different accents—Gandolfini looming over the doll-like Aston, who hits back with a little steel-magnolia bite. "I've made Jell-O that's been harder than your dick," M'Darlin' says. "Aww, c'mon, I was ill! I told you I was sick!" Her spunk elicits a kind of vulnerability out of Bucky. (The kidding about their accents went on into the next century; Aston played a recent phone message for me after James's death in which he mocks her drawl—"Jaaa-iimes, Jaaa-imes, Jaaa-imes, O mah Lawd, today!" was all he said.)

Aston has kept a videotape, from 1988, of one of their *Tarantula* performances. Gandolfini, Aston says, weighed 185 pounds. Thin and slightly round-shouldered, looking a bit more like John Cleese than Tony Soprano, he nonetheless brings an implied forcefulness to his presence that jumps off the screen.

Gandolfini had just graduated from Kathryn Gately's class when he met Aston, and he urged her to take a six-week study with his teacher, which she did. Then they started to work together to develop elaborate backstories for their showcase characters. As they worked out scenes they collected stage notes that shaped their performances.

In a way, it was a sketch of the ideal character James thought he could portray. He wrote out an outline in long-hand, in blue marker on white lined paper, describing who Bucky's father and mother were, what they did for a living, what Bucky hoped to become. It described the conflicts that shaped his personality. Aston still has it, and the one she made for M'Darlin'. They were alternate identities—he was using his self-christened college nickname, for pete's sake—recreated for the stage. There was some shaman-like authenticity in that.

Gandolfini did other acting gigs wherever he could, often for no pay. His first film appearance in a speaking role was shot in 1989 as a student project at New York University. David Matalon, who was studying filmmaking, scraped together $10,000 to make *Eddy,* about a working guy who falls in love with a prostitute, Madge. Her pimp, Mike, played by Gandolfini, decides to put a stop to Eddy's plans to take Madge out of the business and shoots him, inadvertently killing Madge, too.

After Gandolfini's death, Matalon told CNN he interviewed fifteen actors for the part before Gandolfini. "None of them were very convincing and threatening," Matalon recalled, "and then he just had it. . . . You could see there's a slight dangerousness in him. It kept it exciting."

That he could bring that kind of intensity to the stage made him stand out. But it was with Aston that Gandolfini kept honing the character he wanted to project, the working-class Everyman whose feelings were both tender and explosive. They did other plays, like *The Danger of Strangers,* in which Aston portrayed a woman who lures Gandolfini's character back to her apartment and kills him. The plotlines tended to hover around the big guy with feet of clay, who knows he can scare people but wants to be loved at the same time.

Gandolfini and Aston's acting dynamic fit one play in the American canon perfectly: Tennessee Williams' *A Streetcar Named Desire. Streetcar* features its own linguistic duet between Polish tough guy Stanley Kowalski and the lilting Southern pretensions of Blanche DuBois. And it was to *Streetcar* that the path begun by *Tarantulas* led. While they were still working on the showcase, Gandolfini got his first real paying job in the theater, playing Mitch, Blanche's aborted suitor, in a production of *Streetcar* set to tour Scandinavia. Sweet, stable Mitch was the Karl Malden part from the movie version of *Streetcar* (Gandolfini would alternate between Mitch and Stanley types in his character roles for years to come).

Gately remembers Jim coming back to her conservatory to tell her he'd just landed his first acting gig. He'd done all sorts of jobs after managing Private Eyes—construction, a little home carpentry, bartending, and bouncing. He once said he sold books on the street. He worked for a long time for a Jewish businessman whose company, Gimme Seltzer, delivered big bottles of the stuff to restaurants and shops around the city. Jim was supposed to start a job cutting down trees when *Streetcar* was offered. Touring Sweden was a lot better than sawing wood.

"I remember lots of old people falling asleep in dinner theaters," is how Gandolfini recalled his tour later, but the trip was definitely an eye-opener. He visited the Van Gogh Museum in Amsterdam, and the Louvre in Paris; when the tour was over, he rolled around Ireland for a week with a girl he'd met through a friend in New Jersey.

When he got back to New York City he did a small part in *One Day Wonder* at The Actors Studio, and in 1991 he took a big part in *Summer Winds*, by Frank Pugliese, performed with the Naked Angels. Marisa Tomei was the star of this "romantic drama in which love songs become love stories" (a premonition of 2005's *Romance & Cigarettes*)—it was his first paying job that used his choir-trained singing voice. *Summer Winds* had two-week runs at a number of different venues, some of them college theaters.

Then, in 1992, he was called back for *On the Waterfront* with The Actors Studio. Gandolfini was cast as Charley, the Rod Steiger part, a major role. But he was abruptly fired after just a week. Some friends remember him scaring people on the set—something about putting his hand through a glass window in frustration, like breaking that security barrier at Rutgers ("He took out his anger on inanimate objects all the time"). Years later Jim remembered it as a "lovely discussion" with one of the producers. A few minutes later, "I got a call telling me I was fired for being too mouthy."

Later that year he got his first real break, playing Steve, one of Stanley's poker pals, in a Broadway production of *A Streetcar Named Desire* featuring the movie stars Alec Baldwin and Jessica Lange. Aida Turturro played Steve's wife, Eunice. Jim would be understudying Mitch. Aston got one of the other poker wife parts. Gandolfini knew the casting director, who lived across the street from his apartment—but there was little question he knew the play. And being part of a Broadway production of *Streetcar* was where his study for the past five years had been leading, almost inevitably, all along.

Streetcar is the arc of inarticulate male longing that sails through American theater in the last half of the twentieth century. With *On the Waterfront*, it's also the fountain from which Marlon Brando's career, and by proxy all postwar working-class method actor careers, springs. And the play carries a deep insight for men who want to act.

Much later, after *The Sopranos* became a hit, Gandolfini put it this way, in an interview with *Rolling Stone*:

> *"I think Marlon Brando said, 'The character that suffers is always the best character in the play'. . . . So people watch Tony, and they watch his mother giving him shit and his wife giving him shit. Even his girlfriend throws shit at him, you know. So here's this powerful figure getting abused all the time, and I think people get a good laugh out of that."*
>
> *And I guess anguish is more fun to play than some chirpy. . . .*
>
> *"I don't know if it's more fun to play, but it's certainly more fun to watch."*
>
> *You think maybe it's not more fun to play?*
>
> *"I think it's a hard character to play, especially over a period of time. Everyone's yelling at you all day long."*

Like *Streetcar*, *The Sopranos* would be a production about the male beast caged, regulated and, at least partly, tamed by women in his family. And about the pathos of so much power so completely overmatched by emotions he can barely express. But all that was still to come. First he had to start going a little Hollywood.

"And after that," Aston says, "he went off to Hollywood with the boys, and I didn't work with him for four or five years."

5.

Character Actor Years: Working-Class Hero vs. Gentle Hitman

Gandolfini actually started his film career in New York, appearing in small parts in several films before he moved away from the theater and "went off to Hollywood with the boys." If you're in a generous mood, you could say his film career began in 1987 with walk-ons, like his role in the low-budget *Shock! Shock! Shock!*, in which he appeared as a hospital orderly. After playing the pimp in the 1989 student film *Eddy*, he took a part so small that it went uncredited in the 1991 Bruce Willis thriller *The Last Boy Scout*, and you had to look quick to catch him as a hood who tries to extort protection money from Hasidic jewelers in Sidney Lumet's 1992 *A Stranger Among Us*, starring Melanie Griffith.

And then, in 1993, he landed the role of Virgil in *True Romance*.

Actually, he was in three movies that year. In *Money for Nothing*, which was shot in Philadelphia, he played the older brother of John Cusack, an out-of-work longshore-man who picks up $1.2 million that fell off an armored car in the middle of the street and then tries to take the money and run. In *Italian Movie* Gandolfini played a young version of Tony Soprano, a small-time neighborhood gambler and sexual predator. He was the chief villain of the film, and he lip-handles a cigar in a way Tony would later do every week in the opening credits for *The Sopranos,* but it was a flawed picture (even with Rita Moreno's cameo). When Gandolfini became famous as Tony Soprano, the production company tried to repackage the film with a big photo of James, but his was really a supporting role.

True Romance was the standout, and not just because of the cast (Gary Oldman, Christian Slater, Brad Pitt, Dennis Hopper, Christopher Walken, Tom Sizemore, Chris Penn, and, of course, Patricia Arquette). For fans, *True Romance* is the first picture in which Gandolfini's range as an actor was finally there to see. It even has a nifty subplot (not involving Gandolfini's character, unfortunately), about trying to make it as a character actor in L.A.

For the people who knew Buck in life, however, it was almost a disappearing act.

"I swear to God, I saw him in that movie and I didn't recognize him," says Mark Di Ionno, the columnist for *The Star-Ledger* who drove Gandolfini to summer stock tryouts after freshman year at Rutgers. "I hadn't seen him for ten years at that point, and man, he'd changed."

We've already described the balletic beating Gandolfini gives Patricia Arquette in *True Romance,* and the ordeal of filming that twelve-minute scene over five days. It says something about Gandolfini's courtliness, and maybe about his sense of gender stereotypes, that he begged Aston not to go see it (she still hasn't). Gandolfini is brutal and terribly convincing in that scene. What gave the beating its dramatic punch, however, was the writing by Quentin Tarantino.

William Goldman, who wrote the screenplay for *Butch Cassidy and the Sundance Kid,* once described that entire movie as a series of reversals of audience expectations. Almost from the beginning, the film sends up the conventions of previous horse operas about the Hole-in-the-Wall Gang: The heroes are betrayed by their trusty sidekicks, the posse doesn't give up when the going gets rough, Butch actually welcomes the bicycle as a potential replacement for his horse—scene after scene upending stereotypes and updating the western in the process.

Quentin Tarantino writes that way, too, only more so. The big reversal in Gandolfini's scene is, of course, that Arquette shoots him with his pistol-grip shotgun at the end. But each little segment along the way twists expectations, too—Arquette doesn't wail and beg for mercy, Gandolfini doesn't just kill her when he finds the suitcase, the tiny corkscrew he mocks becomes an effective weapon, and so on. And until he feels that corkscrew bore into his foot, Gandolfini wears a tight but playful smile that became almost the actor's trademark. He does wince-worthy things throughout the scene, like putting a pretty girl through a glass shower door, for example. And the biggest reversal of all is how we feel about him for it.

Virgil is not a leading character, and he isn't on screen for very long, but he's unforgettable because of that genial air of menace. It's almost a meta performance in that way, a picture of an actor *enjoying* his twists on other actors playing heavies. When Virgil's anger is loosed, it's thrilling because we've been waiting for it, almost hoping for it, to clear the air of ambiguity. And the premonition of Tony Soprano is unmistakable.

"The boys" in that film are all, more or less, graduates of what we might call the *Streetcar* school of male sexuality (Gary Oldman is an exception, perhaps, but is Joe Orton really so different from Tennessee Williams?). Slater is the only real romantic lead. The rest are character actors who, here and there, had breakthrough roles that made them leads—usually roles that allowed them to show an unexpected tenderness or courage or vulnerability.

The Hollywood tradition of turning tough guys into leads is venerable, beginning, you could say, with Humphrey Bogart and Jimmy Cagney, and continuing through Lee Marvin, Warren Oates, Charles Bronson, and on and on. Maybe we should think of it as an inevitable kind of type reversal that comes after committing X number of murders on the screen. *True Romance* put Bucky's foot firmly on that ladder (even though, without getting all Anthony Weiner about it, he didn't actually murder anyone in *True Romance*). There was no guaranteed career, exactly, but you could not mistake the ladder presented. Combined with that physical fearlessness he displayed again and again as a young man, and the affability that won him friends wherever he went, Gandolfini might have seemed a good bet to become a star even when he had so few credits to his name.

Anyway, after *True Romance*, acting really seemed like a grown-up career choice for a thirty-two-year-old single guy. Gandolfini wasn't ready to quit any part-time day job quite yet, but he at least felt sure enough to actually rent a place to live on the West Coast, too. He had started signing leases for his own apartments in Brooklyn and Manhattan in 1989. In 1994, he rented a place in Malibu (he would rent apartments in Sherman Oaks the next year, and a house from 1996 to 1998 in Mount Olympus, in the Hollywood Hills, but he never changed his official residency from New York City throughout his career). For five years he bounced from one coast to the other and from Tennessee to Boston to Florida to the south of France, depending on the production.

Wherever the movies were set, Gandolfini alternated between playing thoughtful, reluctant, bipolar, or just plain likable brutes, and portraying average working-class guys for whom violence was contemptible, or at least, unthinkable.

Sometimes he played characters that weren't killers, exactly, but brought a similar kind of animal ferocity to the screen. In *Le Nouveau Monde*, released in the states as *The New World* in 1995 but shot much earlier, he played an army sergeant with American occupying forces in 1950s France who likes to pick fights with blacks but loves jazz. He helps a sixteen-year-old kid from Orléans learn to play drums "like Gene Krupka" even as he seduces the boy's local girlfriend and goes into an alcoholic tailspin. It's a major if little-known performance, one of his first near-leads, in a French-based production directed by Alain Corneau and costarring Alicia Silverstone. Gandolfini completely dominates the film, showing off his peculiar mix of menace and likability—and standing in for American culture in a way he wouldn't again until Tony Soprano.

One year after *True Romance* comes *Terminal Velocity*, starring Charlie Sheen. Gandolfini played Ben Pinkwater, a seemingly mild-mannered district attorney who turns out to be a violent Russian mobster, a brute in disguise.

That same year, in 1994, Gandolfini took the part of Vinnie, the rejected suitor to Geena Davis, in *Angie*, a twisted romantic comedy. Based on the novel *Angie, I Says*, by Avra Wing, which was listed as a notable book by *The New York Times* in 1991, *Angie* does serious damage to the conventional Hollywood happy ending. Vinnie is a plumber—there's a *Home Improvement*–style send-up of early housing-bubble hardware commercials that gives Gandolfini one of his first comic bits in a movie—and a loyal Bensonhurst boyfriend who can't understand why she won't marry him. Especially since Angie is pregnant with his child. Instead, she has a fling with an international lawyer she meets in the Metropolitan Museum of Art, who of course rabbits when she goes into labor.

It's a story about love and class and being a single mother, and about deciding to stay single even though there's a perfectly suitable husband-in-waiting right in front of you.

Susan Aston says she never saw *Angie,* either—Jim told her Vinnie didn't need any backstory preparation because he'd already done it, with her, in *Tarantulas Dancing.* Shot in New York City, *Angie* had the same sort of dynamic as Bucky and M'Darlin', in the sense that the male character is shocked to find the girl rejects him, and then struggles to accept it. "I was always so happy for him for his success," Aston says, "but that was hard. Not now—now I love teaching acting [she is on the full-time faculty at The Actors Studio Masters of Fine Arts program, which is part of Pace University in lower Manhattan], but then, for a while, it was."

Vinnie was a major part, the biggest Gandolfini had landed to date in an impressive production with Hollywood stars, with real sympathy for a working-class guy. It was the kind of role he'd always wanted, and in a big-budget movie that is actually pretty successful as a drama.

But the movie didn't do as well as expected. Young women, including single mothers, didn't like Geena Davis leaving her sick baby to search for her own mother at the end of the movie. And they just couldn't understand why, when she comes back and devotes herself to raising her child, she doesn't just accept Vinnie, too. Like, what was wrong with big, sweet, lovable, rock-solid James Gandolfini?

Maybe, the audience decided, there was something wrong with Davis.

Angie was a preview of what Gandolfini could bring to a movie, and the effect he could have on an audience well beyond the confines of the script. Even though it was something of a disappointment financially, *Angie* went a long way toward making James a star. Not quite a romantic lead, but certainly a serious character actor.

His way of celebrating was to rent a really big beach house at Mantoloking, on the Jersey Shore, for the summer of 1994, and invite everybody he knew for a month-long party.

T.J. Foderaro came down. He was about to begin working as a wine critic. It was the last time they really hung out. T.J. remembers getting phone calls from Jim on the West Coast afterward, often at two thirty or three o'clock in the morning, around midnight in L.A. T.J. would tell Jim he had to work the next day. Could they talk in the morning some time? The phone would just click off.

If the nights grew long on the far coast, it had to be heady, anyway. Just a couple of years after *Angie* he's doing scenes with Hollywood royalty like Travolta, Sean Penn, Brad Pitt, Rosanna and Patricia Arquette, even the actor Roger Bart had recommended as a role model, Gene Hackman. Gandolfini didn't take it for granted, though—he was too "grounded," as theater people say, to make that mistake. He's making character actor money, remember, never more than low-to-mid-five figures for any role. When Sidney Lumet called to offer him a part in *Night Falls on Manhattan* in 1996, Jim took the call on his cell phone while planting trees for the city in the sidewalk.

By 1995, Gandolfini seemed on the verge of breaking through. He had major parts in two widely anticipated Hollywood all-star productions: *Get Shorty*, based on the Elmore Leonard novel, and then *Crimson Tide*, a submarine-borne national security thriller starring Gene Hackman and Denzel Washington. He hired a new assistant, a pretty blonde who happened to be between jobs, named Marcy Wudarski. She'd never heard of Gandolfini. Marcy had been working for movie companies for a while, and like Aston, she was a military brat from the South (Florida, if that counts). It wasn't long before the two were dating.

In *Get Shorty*, Gandolfini appears as Bear, a gentle leg-breaker working for drug dealers who wants to be a good father. He gets beaten up twice by New Jersey neighbor John Travolta in the film, and yet comes around to join Travolta's Chili Palmer at the end—quite the character reversal in itself. Bear's change of allegiance is the emotional hinge of the movie, turning on his desire to protect his family, and confirming Chili's defeat of the main villain, played by Delroy Lindo.

Get Shorty was a hit, and Bear (for whom Gandolfini attempted his first southern accent in a film) is one of the most memorable characters in the movie. Even more than *True Romance, Get Shorty* is a meta take on Hollywood success, a send-up of industry hype, the feckless dreamers that feed showbiz sharks, and the grubby details of financing that make it all possible. And it's full of questions about traditional movie stereotypes—like the character of Bear himself.

Crimson Tide should have expanded the triumph of *Get Shorty*. Gandolfini played Lieutenant Bobby Dougherty, a crewman caught in the conflict between his two superior officers. The part carried much of the emotional stress of the plot, not unlike the way Bear in *Get Shorty* prefigured the audience's approval of Chili Palmer. Director Tony Scott wanted Jim to do it right after he was finished working in France on *Le Nouveau Monde*, which gave him very little time to prepare. He'd only read the script through once, weeks before. According to Lennie Loftin, a character actor who befriended Jim in the early 1990s, Jim was worried about getting in front of the camera so soon after flying back to the United States. But he didn't want to disappoint the director of *True Romance*.

Scott made four movies with Gandolfini, and the roles he did for the British director (who committed suicide about a year before Gandolfini's own death) were intrinsic to the kind of star James would become. Unfortunately, Virgil in *True Romance* was not exactly the kind of thing you wanted your mother to see, especially if your mother was like Jim's mother.

"Keeping Mama happy" was more than just Gandolfini's off-hand explanation for why he went to Rutgers. It was a real concern of his, all his life, and a particular sore spot was his choice of career. The slightly formal dignity that his colleagues remarked upon in the jokey and irreverent James probably was handed down from Santa; at the same time, the "Class Flirt" in Gandolfini wanted to be loved for his own insouciance. There was a constant tension.

Once, when a local Florida reporter asked Gandolfini to describe Santa Gandolfini, he simply sat bolt upright in his chair and closed his fist in front of his chest, miming a person of great propriety and dignity. Her family ran a small bar in Milan, and even though she'd been born in New Jersey, she had gone back as a child before the war.

"She went through the war in Italy—I think she was about eighteen when the war happened," Jim said later. "She was going to be a doctor. And everything got all screwed up and she had to come to America. I mean, think about this—this was the forties, and she was going to be a doctor."

At just about the same time Gandolfini got back from France, Loftin had decided to move out to Los Angeles to try his hand at acting. (Loftin has appeared in several major films, including *The Sleeper* and *3:10 to Yuma*.) "He knew I was moving out and called to ask when," Loftin said in an e-mail relayed to me by one of Jim's oldest friends. "I said I was coming out with my bull terrier, Millie, in mid-October. I was planning on sleeping on a couple of couches 'til I found a place, but he told me he'd just arrived for *Crimson Tide* and that he had an extra bedroom in a furnished beach condo on the L.A.–Ventura County line, across from Neptune's Net, and I could stay with him while he did the film."

Neptune's Net is a seafood place popular with bikers and surfers just across the county line in Ventura. It's been a neighborhood landmark for more than a generation. That stretch of the coast highway going north is sort of like the Jersey Shore, but bigger—the straight, flat beach stretching out almost as far as the eye can see in either direction, and in front of you the bright boundless Pacific Ocean, where every night the sun sets in an orgy of golds and purples. It's a very nice place to live, especially in a beachfront condo provided by your production company.

"While we were living there, Jim's parents came out to visit for about a week," Loftin recalled. Jim's two older sisters were already well on their ways to responsible jobs, Johanna with the court system in Jersey and Leta as a corporate executive in the garment trade. "One day we were waiting for dinner to cook—I think a game was on TV—so his mom went out to sit in a chair on the deck in the afternoon sun for a few minutes. She looked so happy and peaceful—and almost relieved—like she was able to absorb it all, and she knew that her boy was doing the right thing with his life and that he was going to be okay. I pointed her out to Jim. He got it."

Crimson Tide opened to positive reviews, and it made money, but the story of conflict between submariners of different generations seemed a bit tired. Still, it was a major role with major stars. Gandolfini bought his first home ever in 1996, a nice apartment in the West Village, but his acting career seemed to slow. He released just one film that year, *The Juror*—it was shot in New York City— starring fellow *Streetcar* veteran Alec Baldwin and Demi Moore.

It's in *The Juror* that we begin to see what you might call the Gandolfini Effect: his performance is so good that it comes close to capsizing the movie. Eddie is a hitman, working with rogue Mafia enforcer Alec Baldwin, but he clearly wants to do it with a minimum of angst. Scare the civilian, sure, but keep it within reason—the victim's cooperation in getting the boss off the hook at his trial is Eddie's real focus.

Baldwin's character seems to enjoy terrorizing Moore for its own sake, and somehow to be lost about whom he really is. But Eddie is a normalizing force. His meeting with Moore in a Brooklyn grocery store, where he confesses he's got a kid himself—as if that absolves him of the horror the mob is putting her through—is fascinating. It's just my job, ma'am, nothing personal; please keep your hands and arms inside the vehicle at all times during the ride and you'll be fine.

It's not true, of course. Nothing the victim does will make her fine. But you get the sense that Eddie really *wants* it to be true.

And critics seemed to notice. Roger Ebert said *The Juror* would have been a much better movie if the entire script had been pitched at the level of Gandolfini's performance.

Then, in early January 1997, Santa Gandolfini died.

Several years later, *The National Enquirer* managed to browbeat Gandolfini into discussing on the record his struggles with cocaine and alcohol in the late nineties. On September 26, 1997, about eight months after his mother died, he was arrested for DUI in Los Angeles. "I was racing someone and I was over the limit," he said, joking that "it was the best French toast I ever had when they woke me up in the Beverly Hills jail."

It was an era when Hollywood stars, particularly male stars, seemed to generate stories about drug abuse and wild behavior as if they were on contract to do so. The problems of Robert Downey, Jr., and *True Romance* costar Tom Sizemore were recurrent tabloid fodder. People who worked with Gandolfini later in his career, when he seemed to have control of his drinking and drug abuse, often casually assumed his problems were similar.

But there's actually very little on the record to confirm that assumption. Gandolfini's bad behavior seemed much more episodic than that, like the mood swings friends noticed in college. And he often seemed deeply repentant when it was over, and moved to surprising generosity to anyone he might have offended or inconvenienced. It's not even certain by any means that these occasional breakouts into substance abuse were the cause of Jim's friends' extraordinary protectiveness.

However much of a problem it was, it didn't interfere with getting back to work. He was a corrupt cop in Sidney Lumet's *Night Falls in Manhattan* (1997), a beguiling rapist in *She's So Lovely* (same year, made from an old script by John Cassavetes and directed by his son, Nick, with Sean Penn and John Travolta), and good cop possessed by the demon Azazel in *Fallen* (1998). All of them were both magnetically dangerous and oddly sympathetic.

He was still alternating these roles with attempts at expanding his character actor credits, too. In 1997, in the "Columbus Day" pilot episode of Robert Altman's six-part TV series *Gun*, Gandolfini was another solid, ethnic working guy (who boasts that "Everything that looks good or tastes good was invented by Italians"). His wife, played by Rosanna Arquette, is secretly cheating on him, and the plot is cleverly fashioned so that Jim shoots her lover without ever finding out about the affair—he's a nice guy *and* a killer, and a bit of an innocent dupe. Later that year he played a Drug Enforcement Administration agent who keeps getting hit by passing vehicles but is never hurt, kind of like Wile E. Coyote, in *Perdita Durango. Durango* was a Spanish production directed by Álex de la lglesia, a sort of horror-crime movie starring Rosie Perez and Javier Bardem. It was one of Jim's first completely comic roles, though it was embedded in a kind of bloody occult-revenge flick.

The film he seemed to care about the most from this period was *A Civil Action* (1998), starring John Travolta and Robert Duvall. Shot in Boston, the movie was based on a real incident of chemical contamination in Woburn, Massachusetts, that established corporate responsibility for poisoning public water supplies. Gandolfini's part was modest but crucial—he plays Al, the first employee of the waste disposal companies working for W. R. Grace and Beatrice Foods to come forward with evidence of improper dumping of carcinogens in the town's watershed. Literally a working-class hero.

Gandolfini may have been thinking about this film when, years later, on *Inside the Actors Studio,* he answered a question about what alternative profession he might have liked to pursue if he hadn't become an actor: "Environmental lawyer."

Still, it was the heavies the movies wanted him to do, the desperate monsters you hoped could be saved but really were already lost. In the melodrama about disabled children *The Mighty* (1998) he played "Killer" Kane, the abusive father of one of the protagonists, and in *8MM* (1999) he was a talent scout for snuff films who is murdered by Nicholas Cage (both characters are thoroughly reprehensible).

Oscar Wilde, who knew something about acting and the theater, once said that neither the state of sin nor that of innocence interested him so much as the moment he passed from one to the other. Gandolfini's gift as an actor is to show us how to dance along the line between good and evil, only to suddenly drive across in a blur of immediacy. Just as he did in Gately's class when he "destroyed all that crap they have on stage." Until that moment, he makes us root for him to control himself, not just because it's scary to see such a big guy lose it, but because he makes you feel how much *he* really wants to keep it together himself.

It pulls your sympathy, but it also makes the viewer complicit with his character, giving even his mundane bad guys an odd resonance.

And it was the résumé that he brought with him to what would become his greatest creation as an actor.

6.

The Sopranos Begins (1999)

When the first episode of *The Sopranos* aired on January 10, 1999, nobody could possibly have foretold what the show would become—a monster hit, driving audiences for serious drama away from movies to cable television (of all places), and the first TV series to earn over a billion dollars in syndication, DVD sales, video game profits, etc. Critical raves rolled in.

That kind of thing made James Gandolfini very nervous.

Susan Aston says Jim "tried to quit every role he ever got." It was indeed almost a tic he had. Even for his work on *The Sopranos*. He stopped in the middle of his audition with David Chase and begged to be allowed to come back and do it again—he said he had an illness in his family, and he just wasn't hitting it right. He didn't even show up for the second audition. Gandolfini apologized and asked if he could come by Chase's house and audition there. Surprised, Chase agreed, and Gandolfini came over and audi-

104

tioned in his garage later that night. He finished the whole scene in one go.

"What happens every time [when you're casting something] is that people come in and read, and they read and they read, and you start to think, This is really badly written, the thing sucks," is how Chase remembered Gandolfini's final audition to *Vanity Fair*'s Peter Biskind. "And then the right person comes in, and it all works. It was pretty obvious that Jim had too much going on for this role to go with anyone else."

But Gandolfini didn't see it that way. "I read it. I liked it. I thought it was good," James said afterward. "But I thought they would have to hire some good-looking guy, not *George Clooney*, but some Italian George Clooney, and that would be that."

Gandolfini's manager and friend Mark Armstrong, who has worked with the agency handling Jim's career since *Angie* in 1994, said it got to be like clockwork. "About a week before a production was supposed to start filming, we'd get a letter, copied to the director, in which Jim would give everybody an out, asking them if they were sure they thought he could do the part. And he'd always include the names of three actors he thought were available who could do a better job."

In an industry as ego-driven as show business, Gandolfini's behavior was, to put it mildly, unusual. You might think it was just a way to ward off the evil eye, you know, to placate Nemesis for a lucky break you might not deserve.

But James really seemed to mean it. Everyone who knew him smiles about his absolute modesty. He almost never watched himself perform in daily rushes (he hated looking at them). He had a hard time seeing in his performances what other people saw; he noticed mostly the flaws. And that didn't change as he got more famous as an actor.

It's particularly difficult for us to sympathize with Gandolfini about his talent because it's so hard to imagine any other actor making a better Tony Soprano. Starting with that iconic first episode—Tony wading into his swimming pool in his bearish white terrycloth bathrobe to commune with the wild ducks—he just seemed perfectly suited to the role, physically and emotionally.

"The thing about actors is, when they're really great, they have no idea when they do great work," says Harold Guskin, who helped coach Gandolfini for most of his film roles.

"The Great Guskin," as John Lahr called him in *The New Yorker*, has been coaching actors for some twenty-five years, starting with Kevin Kline, who met Guskin in the 1970s when they were both musicians at Indiana University in Bloomington. Guskin's approach isn't method, but more personal; the idea is to help actors "stop acting" and deliver immediate emotions as if they were immersed in real life. His 2005 book, *How to Stop Acting*, includes quotes from clients like Kline, Glenn Close, Bridget Fonda, and, of course, James Gandolfini.

"Acting has to come from the gut," says Guskin, slapping his still-flat middle. "You don't act with your head. You have to deliver your lines as if they are spoken in real time, in real life. Immediacy is the object. So an actor who is doing really great work *should* have no idea how well he's doing. It's over too quick for him to know.

"And then after acting comes the questioning of everything you did," he continues. "The second thoughts, the self-doubt. It's horrible. Being an actor is very difficult. The pressure . . . can be tremendous."

Many actors have self-esteem issues long before they go on stage; in fact, that's why some are there in the first place, to get unqualified approval from an abstract group of people who don't really know them. Still, even for the best, how they do what they do can be a psychological puzzle. "Some actors are embarrassed by acting," says Nicole Holofcener, who directed Gandolfini in his last feature film, the realistic romantic comedy *Enough Said*. "Just opening their mouths and talking is an embarrassment, and it takes a lot of courage to go on and get through a scene."

Stage actors get an immediate reaction from the crowd, but TV and film acting is mysterious until long after it's been performed, recorded, and edited. So the place of the audience is taken by the director and the crew.

And the crew, as many theater people say, is an idealized family. "It's like a family that you know is going to go through a divorce in three months," Susan Aston says, "except, in the case of *The Sopranos*, the family lasted ten years."

On a lot of TV shows, the star is the head of the "family." In most, the principal actor is much more than just an actor—it's not exactly being the producer, or the director, or the owner of the network, but it's not just reading lines, either. While they were shooting the first season, Gandolfini told one of his closest associates that "it didn't feel right, that he wasn't really a lead actor, that he saw himself differently than that." It was, after all, his first lead since *Tarantulas Dancing*. And yet he went around meeting the other actors and the crew, shaking hands, asking if he could help them in any way, just like a veteran lead.

Jamie-Lynn Sigler, who played Tony Soprano's daughter, Meadow, once told *Rolling Stone* that Gandolfini would get on the phone with her boyfriend and ask him if he was treating her right. She wasn't a child star, exactly, but started on *The Sopranos* as a teenager, and came of age on the set. "He's actually just like a teddy bear," Sigler said of Gandolfini. "I think of him as my second father. You can sit down and have the nicest conversation with him, and then he'll get up and punch walls and beat someone up."

But *The Sopranos* family chart was more complicated than any real family's. David Chase was originally a writer, and in many ways always has been. And writers are not usually at the top of any chart except one made up of other writers. But Chase was a good manager, he'd produced several commercial TV hits, and he changed how writers were viewed in the industry. Through the idiosyncratic success of *The Sopranos,* Chase became the first of a series of "showrunners" who were responsible for creating a new golden age of serious, adult drama on cable TV at the turn of the last century.

And that meant putting great authority in the hands of former writers. Cable dramas are writer-driven because each episode, while containing a ringing climax for its own story, was simultaneously part of a longer arc of thirteen episodes that were supposed to build dramatic tension and provide a satisfying cumulative climax as a finale. This gave TV drama some of the qualities of nineteenth-century serial fiction, like the novels of Balzac, Dickens, and Dostoyevsky, all of which were written to appear in newspapers or magazines.

Like *Les Misérables, The Sopranos* could introduce minor characters that act as leitmotifs inside the larger story, but seem fully rounded dramas all their own; *The Sopranos* could start and drop themes, return to them, and consider them from every possible angle. But to make sense, those many interwoven threads had to be judged for tone from a single viewpoint, and that, in the case of *The Sopranos,* was David Chase's.

Chase had never believed TV could be anything more than a commercial medium. Growing up in New Jersey, he idolized rock stars like Mick Jagger and Keith Richards as the "real artists," who made art out of their everyday experiences without reference to any academy or theory of practice. Behind the camera, he lionized New Wave auteurs and the rebellious European filmmakers of the 1960s whose work defied all convention. For Chase, working in TV was a compromise, because every episode had to have a neat resolution that encouraged viewers to "go out and buy stuff." It was something he did for money, almost a mark of shame.

Cable TV offered an escape from such limitations. HBO didn't sell ads against *The Sopranos*. They sold subscriptions, which were more like movie tickets. Actors could say "fuck" on the air—in fact, they said it so often, and to such hilarious effect, that the writer in Chase worried they were using it too much, like a crutch. Themes that are almost never explored on network television, like the economics of hospital care, or the ambiguities of senile dementia, were fit topics for *The Sopranos*. Chase could use the show to examine aspects of family life that were becoming rare in movies, too.

As creator and showrunner, Chase was the ultimate dad of *The Sopranos,* but at the same time, Gandolfini became his avatar. The extraordinarily talented actor made the scripts come alive; he made Chase's long-running angst about his New Jersey mom—so different from James's deep affection for his own—into art millions could enjoy, even identify with. (Joe Pantoliano, who played Ralph Cifaretto for two seasons, once observed to Peter Biskind that every Italian family he knew was run by these very strong mothers, and that was what struck him about *The Godfather*. In that movie, "everybody is always worried about him," and that seemed totally weird after growing up under his mother's thumb—and then he heard that Mario Puzo had based the character of the Godfather not on his dad, but on his mom, and it all fell into place.)

But as cable dramas spooled out into multiyear events, running the show became a massive job. There were hundreds of employees, costume designers, prop men, photographers, writers for spin-off productions (the video games, for example), and assistants for every one of them, all trying to clear their concerns through the office of the showrunner. He'd conceived the whole show, he'd chosen the actors and the writers, he even said yes or no to how fat an actor was supposed to be (he made Vincent Pastore wear a fat suit until the second season). And yet, he was so busy and preoccupied, he sometimes seemed unreachable.

Is there any other kind of organization—besides an actual family, that is—with such ambiguous lines of authority? Or any other that allows, maybe encourages, such waves of insecurity?

"By the end, I had a lot of anger over things and I think it was just from being tired, and what in God's name would I have to be angry about?" Gandolfini wondered years later to *Vanity Fair*. "The man gave me such a gift in terms of life experience, in terms of acting experience, in terms of money, too. At the beginning, David came to the set a lot, but once it got bigger and it became this thing, you know, he was a little more standoffish. He was harder to talk to. I understand that. The pressure that he had to continue to create, to continue to do great work, was hard. Everybody starts to want something, everybody starts to call, and this one needs this, and can we talk about that? And then there's money, and so you have to pull back and try to protect yourself in a way. I had to learn it and I wasn't very good at it. But then it starts to take its toll. The first couple of years, it was easier. It wasn't such a huge deal. I've said this to him, but maybe not so clearly. I got it. He had to be a little bit of the 'Great and Powerful Oz.' There was no choice."

And as the ultimate cast father figure became increasingly remote, his time budgeted among various constituencies like a Chinese emperor's time was divvied up among court ceremonies, the family members grew anxious. At the same time, the more Gandolfini made the cast and crew his family, replacing Chase as in loco parentis, the more he worried about his ability to deliver for them.

You can easily see echoes of Tony Soprano's problems everywhere, almost like the show was teasing everybody, the actors, the writers, the producers, the network suits, *everybody,* including the viewers, as to what was real and what was art.

Getting whacked became the ultimate symbol of losing the family. Because, for the actors, it was indeed the same thing as getting fired from the family. "Big Pussy" Bonpensiero's death at the conclusion of the second season (Tony discovered he'd become an FBI informant) became the template: The cast took actor Vincent Pastore out for a send-off dinner after his fictional death—a sort of Irish wake for a dead Italian (who wasn't really dead). Many of *The Sopranos'* crew said the day Big Pussy was whacked was the first time they had ever felt serious tension on the set.

And out of that tension, out of that desire to save all the wild ducks who filled the staff and crew of *The Sopranos*, grew a weighty paranoia. *Rolling Stone* told the story this way in 2001:

[Gandolfini] realized what was going on: David Chase was planning to have Tony Soprano whacked. "I had an unusually belligerent day," Gandolfini says, "and I went home and I was sitting there and I was struck with the realization. . . . I said, 'David's going to kill me.'"

The next morning, he called Chase at home. "He said that during the night he was not able to sleep," says Chase, "and he said to me, 'I realized: Oh, shit, I know what he's doing—he's going to kill me off.'" Listening to Gandolfini, Chase realized "something like how much I value this show, how great it's all been. And that it would be entirely possible to do that—would actually make for an interesting surprise. I just felt very warm toward him. And I thought to myself, 'Man, actors, we forget what it's like to be an actor.' How little they have to hang on to, in a way. What they do is so ephemeral.

Here he is, a huge star, the most popular guy, and that he would think that. You know what else I thought? 'That guy's an artist.' Because even if it went through most TV stars' minds, they'd never make that call. Even if it flitted through their mind, they would say, 'Well, I'm indispensable, there's no show without me.' And that's why he's an artist. Theoretically I think we should believe that it could happen. I think if you start to think that Tony is not in jeopardy, that's not a good thing."

Chase told him he was "a fucking lunatic."

This would not be the last time Chase had to tell Gandolfini something like that. In fact, as the show went on, and the accolades for both men kept rolling in, Gandolfini's confidence, if anything, got worse. He'd beg for time off, miss takes, sometimes disappear for a day, two, even three, when he had some difficult scene that required an emotional push.

It happened because it was good. Because everyone working on *The Sopranos* knew they had lucked into that sweet place where they had freedom, money, control, and an audience for everything they did. For an artist, it doesn't get better than that.

It doesn't get worse, either.

In a show about family, if it's going to be true to life, everything will be about compromise.

The character of Tony Soprano was hemmed in by his families: nuclear, extended, and criminal, and by the much larger dysfunctional family of his country, which was attacked on September 11, 2001, just as *The Sopranos* was hitting its stride. The show at first seemed to be about American economic dysfunction: the only families that make it in middle-class America anymore have to be doing something illegal, or anyway something that should be illegal. But as America went on a ten-year-long hunt to whack enemies and disloyal allies around the world, the footprint of *The Sopranos* inevitably grew.

That was in the accordionlike nature of what David Chase had created. A satire of American family life would naturally reflect all the changes shaping the larger culture, just as Carroll O'Connor had reflected the working class's conversion to Ronald Reagan on *All in the Family* or Homer Simpson reflects the obesity epidemic (and so much else) on *The Simpsons*. *The Sopranos* would adapt itself to reality like a vine does to the stake it curls around—this kind of average family depiction is what TV has always done best. But the process of creating a cable series had another layer of complexity. The show would adapt itself to the qualities brought to it by its lead actor, too.

In the very beginning, when Chase was talking with Fox TV about developing the show, Broadway star Anthony LaPaglia (who won a Tony for his role in *A View from the Bridge* in 1998) was the leading candidate to play the mob boss on Prozac. But LaPaglia couldn't commit, and in the end Fox passed, as all the broadcast networks did. When finally HBO gave the greenlight in 1998, Chase brought three actors to the company as possible Tony Sopranos: Steven Van Zandt, former guitar player for Bruce Springsteen's E Street Band, character actor Michael Rispoli, who'd played Aida Turturro's husband in *Angie*, and James Gandolfini.

Chase had been intrigued by Little Stevie Van Zandt after watching his speech for the induction of The Rascals into the Rock and Roll Hall of Fame on VH1, but HBO was worried about him because he'd never acted before. Van Zandt wound up, of course, as Tony's consigliere, nightclub impresario Silvio Dante. Rispoli was thought to be much funnier than Gandolfini, more charming. But that wasn't ultimately what Chase was looking for—Rispoli took the part of the Jersey don dying of cancer in the early episodes, whose death clears the way for Tony's rise.

"The show I envisioned is the show that's got Jimmy in it," Chase told Alan Sepinwall for his book, *The Revolution Was Televised: The Cops, Crooks, Slingers and Slayers Who Changed TV Drama Forever*. "It's a much darker show with Jimmy in it.

"At one time, I had said that this thing could be like a live-action *Simpsons*," Chase continued. "Once I saw him do it, I thought, 'No, that's not right. It can be absurdist, it can have a lot of stupid shit in it, but it should not be a live-action *Simpsons*."

It was the astonishing immediacy of Gandolfini's temper that made him stand out (one of producer Brad Grey's assistants had sent Chase that twelve-minute clip from *True Romance* before the auditions). But it was the way he tried to stifle his anger, to keep it from breaking out, that made the part perfect for him. Gandolfini was unmatched in his ability to show bridling impatience with his loved ones turn almost instantaneously into heartfelt sympathy. He was a poet of the emotional burdens of long-term loyalty. He *wanted* to be a perfect dad. In just the worst way.

And that was another stake for the vine to curl around, because the success of *The Sopranos* echoed through Gandolfini's personal life, and in several different ways.

For one thing, it meant a serious boost in his income. Remember, just two years before he tried out for the part of Tony, when Sidney Lumet called Jim to offer the role of a corrupt cop in *Night Falls in Manhattan*, Gandolfini was working a part-time job planting trees in the sidewalk when he took the call on his cell. A TV series meant steady work. More work, as it turned out, than anyone expected. He stood to make more money in the first year than he had on all his movies combined.

Gandolfini was thirty-eight years old when he auditioned for Tony Soprano, getting into middle age by most definitions. Yet he had not had the lead in a film or TV program until Tony Soprano came along. And even then, *The Sopranos* was not a network show. Back in 1999, the big earners on TV were network comedians, like Ray Romano, Kelsey Grammer, and Tim Allen who was pulling down $1.6 million per episode of *Home Improvement* as early as 1996. The quartet on *Friends* were getting $750,000 an episode by 2000, and as much as $1 million per by 2002.

Cable pay was more modest, though it certainly beat planting trees. For the first season of *The Sopranos*, Gandolfini was paid $55,000 an episode, a little more than $650,000 for the season. In 1999 he appeared in just one movie, *8MM*, a thriller about snuff films starring Nicholas Cage, which got disappointing reviews. He'd signed a standard five-year contract with HBO, but as was pretty common in the business, the company bumped his salary for the second season when they saw the show was a hit (it's not entirely clear, but guesstimates of $200,000 per episode have been made). Gandolfini released no movies in 2000, when he concentrated almost exclusively on Tony Soprano.

David Chase was in the same boat. Although he was given $100,000 for the pilot script, his starting salary as showrunner in 1999 was around $50,000 to $60,000 per episode.

Gandolfini had to welcome the money. In 1999, James was deciding to start a family in real life, too, for the first time, with Marcy Wudarski.

Marcy was born Marcella Ann Wudarski in 1967. She came from a military family, and graduated in 1981 from Bayonet Point Junior High School in Hudson, Florida. "He was nobody when we met," Marcy told the *New York*

Post much later. "I was between jobs, working for a movie company, and a friend suggested I be a part-time helper, do some piddling things for 'this actor you never heard of who's made a couple of nothing movies.'"

They'd been a couple since 1997. When *The Sopranos* started, Marcy had already moved into the West Village apartment James had bought in 1996. He added an adjoining apartment as *The Sopranos* started, and started furnishing it with stuff they'd picked up in big-box stores. They had a son, Michael, later in 1999. James's two families would grow together, on camera and off.

Shooting an episode for the first season of *The Sopranos* was something like shooting that twelve-minute fight scene in *True Romance* over five days. Except *The Sopranos* was shooting a fifty-minute episode over eight days, with dozens of interacting characters on several different sets and outdoor locations.

The same SAG rules applied—actors had to have twelve hours between a wrap and the next day's start, so each hour you run over one day adds an hour to when you finish the next. By the end of the week, days no longer begin or end—they're figments of the Gregorian calendar.

A cable "season" is shorter than a network season—*The Sopranos* did thirteen hour-long episodes most seasons, compared to a network's twenty-two to twenty-four episodes a year. A network sitcom clocks in at twenty-two minutes an episode, an hour-long drama usually at forty-four minutes an episode. Cable dramas are longer and more variable, lasting anywhere from forty-five to fifty-five minutes. (That means a comic with a hit network show actually puts in about as much screen time in twenty-four episodes as *The Sopranos* did in twelve.) During its first season, *Sopranos* episodes were shot in eight days, a breakneck pace compared to those in the final season, which took as much as twenty-eight days to shoot.

James had kept the practice of developing character notes for each of his roles, writing them down in a notebook, just as he had done with Susan Aston for *Tarantulas Dancing*. The notebooks were filled with social background, family details, bits of memory, what acting coach Harold Guskin calls "incredibly complex, just dozens of alternative" histories for each character he was to portray. Gandolfini would copy out bits of dialogue and then write notes about what the character was thinking when delivering those lines, what he knew or did not know that would influence how he said them.

Memorization became a big problem, just like it was so many years ago at Park Ridge High. Gandolfini was in almost every scene. During shooting weeks he had to memorize more dialogue in less time than he ever had before. When they were working on the fifth episode, "College," cowritten by Chase and James Manos, Jr., in which Tony takes his daughter Meadow to tour potential colleges,

Gandolfini hit a wall. Or, better put, he hit a phone booth, as he told Peter Biskind in 2007:

I had never done anything like that amount of memorization in my life. I'm talking five, six, seven pages a night. David might have regretted giving me his home phone number, because I'd wake him up at three thirty in the morning and say, "What the fuck, man?! You're fuckin' killing me! I can't do this. I'm gonna go crazy!" Like I had to do almost a one-page monologue in a phone booth. And being the calm person that I am—especially then—I couldn't get it. I'd forget my lines. I took the phone, and I smashed it a couple times. After that, I broke the windows in the phone booth. Crack! Smash! Bang! And all I could hear was David laughing hysterically. And then I started laughing. And I said, "You know, I can't memorize all this shit." But you learn, you learn how to do it.

The rest of the cast knew it was Gandolfini's performance that made the show work, and most of them understood the intense pressure he had to be under. "He was a great actor, man, a great actor," Tony Sirico told me. "I watched him like a hawk. The way he'd give a line and then take a breath, look at you, like he was thinking it over. . . . He worked so hard, that Jimmy. I did the 'Pine Barrens' [the 2001 episode in which Christopher Moltisanti and Paulie Walnuts take a Russian mobster out into a frozen forest and shoot him, chase him, and then get lost in the snow]. I was in thirty scenes—thirty scenes! I lost like ten pounds. And Jimmy did that every week."

"Some of that turmoil that's inside of Jim, that pain and sadness, is what he uses to bring that guy to the screen," Chase once said about the phone booth incident. "He'd complain, 'These things I have to do [as Tony], I behave in such a terrible way.' I'd say to him, 'It says in the script, "He slammed the refrigerator door." It didn't say, "He destroys the entire refrigerator!" You did that. This is what you decide to bring to it.'"

Chase laughed again. "The reason I was amused [when he destroyed the phone booth] is because I have these same tendencies as he does, which is I'm very infantile about temper tantrums with inanimate objects. Telephones and voicemail menus, that sort of stuff drives me crazy."

So much of acting is about discipline, concentration, and preparation, combined with endless sitting around and waiting, that it seemed almost designed to challenge Gandolfini's temper. And that might be why the guy who never backed away from a physical challenge was so drawn to it in the first place. "I yell when I can't put shit together," Gandolfini told *GQ* many years later. "When you've got to screw little fucking screws into little things, like putting a table together. I start screaming, 'This fucking crap . . .This shit . . . Fucking Japanese shit . . .' Like that.

"I used to have to put Ikea furniture together when we

were first married and had the baby. All that Ikea shit. I used to swear and yell. So occasionally I'll have that Italian 'fucking' fit. Which is funny. I mean, I've had some good laughs at my father's fits.

"But then, some ain't so funny."

If shooting a cable drama in eight days seemed to drive middle-aged men on high-protein diets to apoplexy, the structure was often like putting together an Ikea end table. Nothing is shot in sequence, of course. The actor doesn't see the finished product, only all the pieces scattered around him. If you're playing a supporting role in a film, with a discrete few pages of dialogue and one, maybe two tricky action shots, it can be easy to keep track of your character development from scene to scene. But for a weekly drama, especially one with as many moving parts as *The Sopranos*, just knowing who you were from shot to shot was an achievement.

James had called Susan Aston when he got the part. He knew he'd be in New York City much more consistently for a while, so that was good. As he had for years, he'd discuss character issues with her, go over scenes, and trade suggestions and acting tips. They talked about scenes in the pilot, about Tony as a character, and about the scripts, which they both thought were just the "best writing in the world."

One thing led to another, and Aston started to keep notes for every scene, story, and episode on her computer. Above and below each passage of dialogue she'd type in notes for Gandolfini about what the character knew, felt, had said or would say about this point in the story. There'd be questions about how he felt about the characters he shared the scene with, too—like, "Does Tony think Christopher is too undisciplined for this honor?"

At first, it was informal. "I worked with him on the pilot, but we didn't know that would go anywhere," Aston recalls. Aston was already pretty busy, teaching acting at Pace University, every Monday through Thursday from 2:00 to 5:00 P.M. They were sort of assuming that as the role went on, James would be able to wing it more. And then, early in the first season, James destroyed the telephone booth when he couldn't remember his lines. And the production decided to hire Aston.

"I didn't get paid until the third episode," she says. "They listed me as 'dialogue coach,' because I couldn't be an *acting* coach, you couldn't say that. It's not that he needed someone to teach him how to play Tony, but he did need someone to collaborate with on the overwhelming amount of actor's homework he had every night."

Aston became the keeper of Tony Soprano's psychology. James told Aston she was "his Dr. Melfi" when it came to putting the character on the screen.

"The actor always knows more than the character," Aston explains. "You know, if you have a big fight with your wife and you have to leave the house before you can make peace with her, all day long that need is working on your unconscious, even if you're not thinking about it or even aware of it. But an actor has to look at the whole story all the time. An actor has to put that mechanism in place, so that when he expresses the character you can see it."

And *The Sopranos* really was about one character, with all the supporting characters funneled through his head: Tony.

"On the set of *The Sopranos,* they called us an old married couple," Aston says, "because after a day's shoot, James was never free to just go off with the other actors. Todd Kessler [a friend of James's and a writer and cocreator of the FX series *Damages*] came to me at the wake and said, 'I can't tell you the number of times when I was out with James and I heard him say, "Ahhh, I can't, I gotta go work with Susan Aston."'" Because we were there night after night when a day's work was done for everyone else, going over eight or ten pages of dialogue for the next day. . . . We had to, in order to be prepared. Never mind memorizing all that."

Gandolfini had his own system for memorizing his lines—writing his cues on one side of a 3 × 5 note card and his lines on the other. At the heart of the Meisner method of acting, you'll remember, is listening—responsiveness to other actors. That had always been the dynamic of their acting together, that duet of accents. Bucky leaning over M'Darlin' to get inches from her face and try to overwhelm her, M'Darlin' standing up to him but evasively, maddeningly, never saying exactly what she meant. Maybe a little like Nancy Marchand as Livia Soprano. But more like the North invades the South and gets lost somewhere in the bayous. Think, again, of *A Streetcar Named Desire*.

And out of that came the sense of a man caged, haltered, powerful but trying to balance a dizzying array of conflicting loyalties. A man who hurts others out of his own pain, who wants to stay loyal to his own family while setting the worst example for them because of who he can't help being. A family guy whose job demands he cheat and brutalize a succession of other families in his life no matter what he wants to do. Stanley rapes Stella's sister Blanche every night, twice on matinee days.

Preparation was Gandolfini's secret sauce, the craftsmanship he brought to every project that justified his contribution. Gandolfini once told Brad Pitt—"because I couldn't think of anything else to say"—that he felt he was so lucky just to be there—the son of immigrants, sharing the camera with people like Pitt, or Gene Hackman. Or Lorraine Bracco, for god's sake, who'd once had a child (and a famously unhappy break-up) with Harvey Keitel, the star of *Mean Streets,* one of James's favorite movies.

Pitt told him he wasn't lucky, he'd "worked his ass off" to get there, just as he himself had. The quality of the work was proof.

The Sopranos crew had only an inkling that first season of the alchemy that they were committing. Or that in the years to come James Gandolfini would become more than an avatar for David Chase. Chase called Gandolfini a

"Mozart," with no idea of how brilliant his acting was—like Mozart, Jim was still basically a little boy.

One of the classic stories about Jim on the set of *The Sopranos* became the "hula dance" he'd do to distract Bracco during her close-ups. When she was supposed to be listening to Tony Soprano as Dr. Melfi with a wise or at least noncommittal seriousness on her face, Jim Gandolfini would occasionally be standing next to the camera, mooning her.

"We had no idea, we were just so busy doing our work," Tony Sirico says. "Then we went over to Italy for the beginning of the second season, to Naples. That's where my people are from. I'm what they call a Napoli don. The Isle of Capri is just a few miles up the coast from there, you know, [he starts to sing,] 'T'was on the Isle of Capri that I found her. . . .' And who do I get to go to Capri with? Big Pussy. Vincent Pastore.

"Anyway, so we get to the island, and we get off the boat and get on the what do you call it, the train up the mountain," he continues. "And so Vincent and I are there in the car, we're just sitting there, and there's like fifteen tourists from Ireland in the car, and we hear them start saying, 'Hey, it's Paulie, that's Pussy!' Like, they know us. Tourists from fucking Ireland know the show! That's when it hit me. This thing was a really big deal."

Some TV shows take a little time to find an audience. But not *The Sopranos*. Overnight, James Gandolfini became one of the most recognizable American actors in the world. He certainly couldn't hide: he was six feet tall and, at the beginning of the show, some 265 pounds. Is anyone ever prepared for the way celebrity can upend their sense of self? Some people, like those whose parents work in the entertainment business, have at least seen it in their regular lives. People like Robert Downey, Jr., say, or Jeremy Piven.

Gandolfini wasn't like them. He'd already lived more than half—more like three-fourths—of his life before celebrity happened to him. One of the strangest things to Jim was the way his character could do the most horrible things (like garrote a Mafia snitch he sees while taking Meadow on that tour of colleges, an act so gruesome HBO executives pleaded with Chase to cut it), and yet the public seemed to love him for it. He was playing a villain, in his words a "New Jersey lunatic." It made no rational sense, like American celebrity itself.

But his incredible popularity was unmistakable. Gandolfini's manager Mark Armstrong tells the story of how, by the middle of the first season, HBO was asking Gandolfini to help out their other big production, Friday night boxing, by coming to the HBO skybox and making an appearance before the fight. Armstrong and his partner, Nancy Sanders, flew out from Los Angeles in March 1999 on business, and Gandolfini asked them to come with him to a Holyfield-Lewis match.

Armstrong says they met in the skybox with a bunch

of people from HBO. And then four security guards showed up and asked Jim to come with them.

"I thought, that's a little unusual," Armstrong says. "People would stop Jim when he was visiting L.A. with me, but it was usually like one or two people, and they'd say things like, 'Mr. Gandolfini, I really respect your work, sir.' But here in New York, somebody had assigned him four security guards—this is going to be different.

"So these guards walk us out into Madison Square Garden. And the whole place erupts, '*To-nee! To-nee! To-nee!!*' And he put his arms around both our shoulders, drew us close, and said, 'See what you've done to my life?'"

It was incredible, it was like a joke. (Other people reported that when he took them out into those cheers at the Garden, he'd lean over and say, "Be nice to me, or I'll have them kill you.") It seemed so far outside his notion of who he was.

The day after that Madison Square Garden crowd scene, Gandolfini did a reading with Meryl Streep for a movie they were considering (it didn't work out). After the reading Mark and Nancy walked Streep and Jim back to her hotel in midtown, and every block, people would recognize him, shout out "Hey, Tony!" or stop them to tell him *The Sopranos* had shot some scene in front of a best friend's house in Jersey or something. Meryl Streep, of course, has been nominated seventeen times and won three Oscars. She is almost universally admired as one of the leading American actors of her generation, a famed technician of character whose ability to inhabit any role has been her hallmark ever since she starred at the Yale Drama Department. And she looked at Jim and said, "How do you do it?"

"What are you talking about?" Jim asked in reply. "You're Meryl Streep. Like, everybody knows you."

Streep looked up at Gandolfini and said, "Have you noticed, they're not yelling at me?"

7.

Troubles on the Set (2000–2003)

Five years after *The Sopranos* ended, scriptwriter Terence Winter, who went on to create the cable series *Boardwalk Empire* about the Jazz Age gangsters who built the Jersey Shore, told *Vanity Fair* that there was a sort of barbershop-mirrors effect to writing about the Mafia.

"One F.B.I. agent told us early on that on Monday morning they would get to the F.B.I. office and all the agents would talk about *The Sopranos*," Winter recalled. "Then they would listen to the wiretaps from that weekend, and it was all mob guys talking about *The Sopranos*, having the same conversation about the show, but always from the flip side. We would hear back that real wiseguys used to think that we had somebody on the inside. They couldn't believe how accurate the show was."

Forget about what the F.B.I. thought of *The Sopranos*. The real point here is that *the mob* thought it was so true that Chase or someone at HBO had to have an inside source—they thought there was a stool pigeon singing in David Chase's ear.

One of the great things about *The Sopranos* was the way it played with fact and fiction. *The Sopranos* had embedded in it an ongoing critique, or maybe parody, of the way reality is depicted by TV. David Chase took delight in mocking the established conventions of dramatic closure and edifying moral lesson that TV had always peddled. His show pretended to realism while depicting a perennial fictional American archetype, the Italian mobster; it became a hit dramatic series, based on wonderfully written scripts, in an era when "reality TV" and (at least putatively) unscripted stories were the hottest innovations in the medium. Untying the knots Chase's series wove between his world and our own became one of the delights fans found so fascinating about Tony Soprano's story.

Chase himself had described the show as *The Simpsons* with guns or *Twin Peaks* in the Meadowlands. He was thinking of the vulgarity of *The Simpsons*, its anarchic parody of the ups and downs of family life as it is usually shown on TV. *The Sopranos* would be a parody of Italian gangster movies, of the sentimental mythic sheen *The Godfather* movies peddled, and of day-to-day suburban life. We'd see Tony Soprano drive to the mall, buy an ax at a gardening center, play golf with his next door neighbor.

Gandolfini said that he'd heard Chase say the show was a story about "people lying to themselves" about who they are.

Gandolfini's performance carried the greatest truth. He seemed to braid reality and art effortlessly. He was, of course, a Jersey guy—even though he needed an accent coach to get that clipped, central Jersey, staccato-Italianese sound. He was gregarious, but he could be moody; he was gently clumsy, sweet, and intuitive about the feelings of others, but he could be forceful when pushed or cornered, like you might expect of a former nightclub bouncer. On the show, when Tony is spotted at the gardening center carrying the ax, his neighbor visibly quakes with fear at the sight. Gandolfini's eyes record first bland suburban bonhomie, then consternation, then realization, followed quickly by a faint hint of anger at his inability to blend into his identity as just another suburban dad. Jim could encapsulate the entire narrative arc of the season in three or four muscle twinges around his oddly transparent, hooded eyes.

The rest of the cast—at least, the rest of the male actors—wanted to get across the same pugnacious authenticity. It came easy to Tony Sirico, who played Paulie "Walnuts" Gualtieri, the Soprano family captain and enforcer: Sirico had been arrested twenty-eight times in his youth, spending seven years altogether behind bars, and claimed to have been offered the chance to be made in the Mafia. He said he'd turned them down because he had "troubles with authority." By the time *The Sopranos* had started he'd been in maybe forty movies and fifty TV shows, almost always playing a mobster or some other kind of heavy.

But everybody started getting into character on the set, and it got hard sometimes to go back to being themselves. Producer Brad Grey said contract negotiations became "testosterone-fueled" as the guys started channeling their characters when they talked with management.

The strangest twists started happening in real life. Michael "Big Mike" Squicciarini played hitman "Big Frank" Cippolina for two episodes of the 2000 season. Then "Big Frank" got whacked, and Big Mike left the show; and then Big Mike himself died in 2001, of natural causes.

Yet even after his two deaths—the fictional one followed by the real one—Squicciarini's name turned up in 2002 in papers filed by Manhattan D.A. Michael Hillebrecht against the Brooklyn branch of the DeCavalcante Mafia clan. The government asserted that Squicciarini, who was six-five and weighed upward of three hundred pounds, had been present when drug dealer Ralph Hernandez was executed by Joseph "Joe Pitts" Conigliaro from his wheelchair back in 1992.

Big Mike wasn't around to defend his good name (given his previous five-year stint in prison for an aggravated assault committed in Monmouth County, New Jersey, his defense might have been flawed in any case). But Squicciarini's posthumous rap sheet justified "former *Sopranos* actor linked to cold-blooded murder" as a media factoid.

Squicciarini's bit part on *The Sopranos* came eight years after a prosecutor alleged he was in the background for a mob rubout, but the story acquired legs when Robert Iler, who played Tony's son, A. J. Soprano, was arrested for robbery and marijuana possession in July 2001. Iler was hanging out with three other teenagers in his Upper East Side neighborhood in Manhattan when they ran into two sixteen-year-old tourists from Brazil. Iler and his buddies demanded their wallets, making off with $40.

The tourists flagged down a passing police car and caught up with the four teens in nearby John Jay Park, sitting on a bench. Iler was sixteen himself at the time. "Life imitates television" was the lede in story after story.

When the posthumous Squicciarini story came out, the media saw a pattern. From then on, no *Sopranos* actor could have a brush with the law without a media ripple. As with Squicciarini, there was no statute of limitations, either. In April 2005, for example—nearly four years after "Big Pussy" Bonpensiero was liquidated on HBO—the actor who played him, Vincent Pastore, was charged with attempted assault on his then-girlfriend, Lisa Regina, in Little Italy, of all places. He ultimately agreed to do seventy hours of community service after pleading guilty to attempted assault, and later settled a civil suit with Regina out of court. Most headlines about Pastore's problem had the word *Sopranos* in them.

Nine months later, the worst imitation of art occurred. Lillo Brancato, Jr., who played aspiring mobster Matthew Bevilaqua, was arrested and charged with manslaughter for an attempted burglary in the Bronx. A police officer, Daniel Enchautegui, was shot and killed when he confronted

Brancato and his accomplice. The partner went to jail for life without parole; Brancato was acquitted of murder charges, but got ten years for first-degree attempted burglary. When Gandolfini died, reporters went to the New York state prison where Brancato was serving time to get his reaction.

No offense was too petty. Near Christmas in 2006, Louis Gross, who played Tony's muscle-bound bodyguard Perry Annunziata, was arrested. Gross was pinched for criminal mischief after a woman said he had tried to break into her house in New York City. (He subsequently received probation.)

Even ending the show didn't stop the stories. In October 2011, more than three years after the last episode of *The Sopranos* aired, John Marinacci was charged with taking part in a "low-level gambling operation in the Gambino Bookmaking Enterprise" along with thirty-six others. Marinacci, who taught poker in real life and had played a dealer in two 2004 episodes of *The Sopranos*, went on to bit parts in *Boardwalk Empire,* too. (His legal responsibility in the gambling case remains unresolved as we go to press.) In December that same year, Anthony Borgese, who had played captain "Larry Boy" Barese on *The Sopranos,* pleaded guilty to arranging the beating of a man who owed money to an upstate car dealership. A Gambino family heavy did the beating, breaking the victim's ribs and jaw. Borgese, who also goes by the stage name Tony

Darrow, got a reduced sentence by agreeing to speak to youth groups about the dangers of mob involvement and film a public service ad.

By the end of the show's run, *The Sopranos* was so synonymous with American organized crime that TV news shows would use the logo—"Sopranos" with an automatic pistol as the "p"—as a symbol for crime news. When New Jersey police broke up a ring of Jewish rabbis who were selling human organs on the black market with mob help in 2009, a New York station actually ran their account over a clip of Tony getting out of his SUV taken from the show's familiar opening credits. Jon Stewart, another Jersey native, devoted a couple of minutes on *The Daily Show* to the ethnic alphabet soup of organized crime his home state had become in the media.

It's hard to interpret this leitmotif in the tabs and Hollywood press without thinking about Italian cultural stereotypes. Just about every immigrant group of any size in America has generated its own criminal subculture: There are Irish mobsters and Jewish mobsters and Lebanese mobsters. Not to mention Hungarian, Chinese, French, and Russian gangsters. Examples show up all the time in the movies; even Gandolfini played a KGB-turned-Russian-mob killer in *Terminal Velocity.*

But Italians are somehow the *real* mobsters, even today. If you go to a strip club in the Russian section of Brooklyn called "Little Odessa," home to local franchises of the Russian Mafia, you'll see nude revues of pretty blond Russian girls dressed (only) in Armani suit jackets and Borsalinos, dancing to a discofied version of *The Godfather* theme. The movies had a lot to do with that—Edward G. Robinson (who was as Jewish as those organ-thieving rabbis) playing *Little Caesar*, deadly but dapper, is a case in point. But as we already noted, the movies enshrined Irish mobsters, too, like James Cagney. Tony Sirico told me that the way Paulie Walnuts holds the pinky ring on his right hand with his left, both arms held out flat in front of his stomach, is his personal homage to Cagney.

Italian-Americans attribute the focus on Italian gangsters to sheer prejudice. "My grandfather never considered himself white. . . ." Italian-American cultural organizations protested *The Sopranos* throughout its run. Some towns along "Guinea Gulch," like Bloomfield itself, refused to allow the show to film in their precincts. All of Essex County public property, including the parks and nature preserves, was declared off-limits for filming *The Sopranos* in 2000 because the county commissioners felt the production showed Italian-Americans in a "less than favorable light." In 2002, after the episode titled "Christopher" tackled questions of Italian-American identity through Newark's annual Columbus Day parade, its organizers officially banned *Sopranos* cast members from taking part. "Come on, you can't poke fun at yourselves," Gandolfini said about this Italo-delicacy. "What is that? You got to be able to poke fun at yourselves. In terms of the violence and things like that, you are damned if you do and damned if you don't. 'Oh, they are making these monsters cuddly and nice,' and then we will do an episode with the stripper where we show what these guys are capable of and the violence is too much. Are you crazy? It's a depiction of these people."

But other towns, often more affluent ones farther along on the northwestern trail to suburban assimilation—like Montclair, Verona, and the Caldwells—embraced *The Sopranos*. Perhaps they understood it was a parody of movie gangsters; maybe they recognized that a hit TV show filmed in their midst would be good for business. Probably they realized that it was just make-believe. If they did, they were right. In August 2001, Fairleigh Dickinson University, in Madison, New Jersey, conducted a national poll that found that 65 percent of Americans disagreed with the statement that *The Sopranos* was portraying Italian-Americans in "a negative way." By the end of the series they repeated the survey and found that 61 percent still disagreed with the idea that Tony Soprano was a negative stereotype.

By then, most of the state had swallowed its objections. Anyway, Bloomfield had. The fade-to-black wrap-up was shot in Holsten's ice cream parlor, one of Bloomfield's better-known eating establishments.

The towns that welcomed *The Sopranos* also subtly acknowledged the élan of being an outlaw culture. It's almost as if the Mafia were the Northeast's version of southern secessionist fantasies: Italian-American culture is fondly portrayed as a law unto itself, outside mainstream American culture, and comfortable with violence as a means to maintain its prerogatives. The *bella figura* of hand-tailored suits and Borsalino hats, Roman Catholicism, and Italian cuisine all exist in opposition to mainstream culture for many Italian-Americans. Especially among men and boys.

Gangster movies do tend to flourish when government is perceived as corrupt or overreaching. *The Godfather* became an antiassimilationist tract for many, an assertion that Italians were not yet melted into the pot. This placed *The Sopranos* at an angle to Italian-American fantasies, in a way. Tony's ongoing difficulties with blending in were funny, but telling, too. The instant he became successful, he would lose his special identity, his livelihood, his family. But he kept trying.

Not everybody recognized the success of the first season. Only Edie Falco took home an Emmy in 1999 (Dennis Franz of *NYPD Blue* won for leading actor in a drama, his fourth, still a standing record). Falco told *Rolling Stone* she remembered stashing the gold statuette in a big tote bag after climbing aboard a cast bus filled with actors who felt slighted.

But HBO knew what they had, and Gandolfini's salary took a nice bump. He'd signed a five-year exclusive deal in 1998. But his value had shot up in Hollywood because of Tony Soprano: in 2001, *The Last Castle*, in which he costarred as a repressed military prison commandant with Robert Redford, earned him $5 million for a supporting role. HBO voluntarily increased Gandolfini's pay from $55,000 per episode to something in the neighborhood of $100,000 in 2000, without negotiations.

Gandolfini won his first of three Emmys in 2000, and after that he signed a new contract with HBO that would give him $10 million for two more (the third and fourth) seasons. His first contract had given him a life-changing financial security, but this, doubling his already bumped salary at one fell swoop, was serious money (though, as his agent said at the time, he was still paid less than Dennis Franz of *NYPD Blue*, Noah Wyle of *ER*, and "every actor but the dog" on *Frasier*). In 2001, he bought a slate-roofed, 150-year-old house on thirty-four acres in Bedminster, in central New Jersey's Somerset County, for $1.14 million. It was in horse country, not far from a home owned by occasional presidential candidate and publishing heir Steve Forbes. Gandolfini told *The Star-Ledger* that his "two-year-old needs to run on grass a little bit."

He bought the $15,000 necklace Marcy wore to the Emmys. He began to indulge his private passion for electronic gadgets (Gandolfini was such a frequent customer at B&H Photo in Manhattan that checkout clerks remember him—he'd happily sign autographs and greet fans while he waited). But he didn't start to collect automobiles, like Jerry Seinfeld, or Art Deco objects, like Barbra Streisand, or Maxfield Parrish paintings, like Jack Nicholson. Friends say as he grew wealthier his biggest splurge would be on time, turning down lucrative acting projects so he could spend time with his family. He rented bigger houses on the Jersey Shore every year.

One thing his success meant right away was better parts in films, and better films, too. In addition to *The Last Castle*, Gandolfini starred in two other movies released in 2001, *The Mexican*, directed by Gore Verbinski and starring Julia Roberts and Brad Pitt, and *The Man Who Wasn't There* by the Coen brothers, starring Billy Bob Thornton. Both are interesting movies, a cut above the commercial razzle-dazzle of *The Last Castle*. Both earned him considerably less than $5 million. But they were good parts, and he was looking for parts that meant something to him more than he was looking for money.

The Man Who Wasn't There is a black-and-white neo-noir movie about murder in a small town and the barber who knows all about it, played by Thornton. Gandolfini played Big Dave, who is running his father-in-law's home furnishing business and may be cuckolding the barber. The role culminates in Gandolfini smashing his office with Thornton's passive-aggressive body until the barber stabs him in the neck with a fake Japanese war trophy, which sounds like an odd reprise of *True Romance*. Jim later said it was a fun scene to shoot because Thornton was "so thin."

Tarted up throughout with a dry-as-the-Gobi sense of humor, *The Man Who Wasn't There* uses Gandolfini's ticking temper to remarkable effect, and stands out as one of the more intriguing movies of his career.

The Mexican could be seen more as an actor's protest against typecasting. Gandolfini played a disillusioned gay hitman named Winston Baldry, who charms Julia Roberts with self-help lore and his own romantic aspirations even as he forces her to help him search for her lover, Brad Pitt, whom he may have to kill. *The Mexican* is the ultimate Gandolfini Effect movie. He is so fascinating, so teetering on the edge between sensitive and lethal, comic and threatening, that when Pitt shoots him three-quarters of the way through the picture it seems as if the heart drops out of the film.

The movie was advertised with the frisson between two of Hollywood's greatest sex symbols, but in fact Pitt and Roberts only had a few scenes together, while the slimmed-down Gandolfini shares the screen with the then-highest-paid actress in the world throughout most of the movie. That was a little like the surprise awaiting *Sopranos* fans who thought they were watching their favorite mob killer in a beard until Gandolfini came out to Roberts in a roadside diner.

Playing a gay hitman was the ultimate reversal on Gandolfini's best-known role. *The Sopranos* took up the theme of a closeted gay wiseguy five years later in its sixth and final season, with the sad story of Vito Spatafore,

played by Joseph Gannascoli. But in *The Mexican* Gandolfini comes out of the closet with a kind of happy shrug—he
and the slightly miscast Roberts undergo the only real psychological development in the movie. Their story so neatly
displaces Pitt's that the Peckinpah-like mytho-comic
fade-out, with its cameo by Gene Hackman, seems like
an afterthought.

Winston Baldry is a character actor's triumph. Julia
Roberts told the press that the way Gandolfini poor-
mouthed his own performance throughout the production
made him a "liar," that he'd been "genius from the start." In
all three of his films from 2001 his characters benefitted
from that dense backstory research that he and Susan
Aston, who worked with him on each of these roles, thought
was a mark of craftsmanship. From little gestures—like
Baldry pressing the tips of his forefinger and thumb together and putting them over his eyes to see what he'd look
like in glasses—to underlying character traits, like his
prison commandant's interest in entomology, Gandolfini
worked to create characters with at least some of the com-
plexities of Tony Soprano.

For two years, James didn't make another movie (his
next picture would be the widely panned comedy *Surviv-
ing Christmas* with Ben Affleck in 2004). There were all
sorts of reasons for that, ranging from working harder for
those two years on *The Sopranos* than he ever had before,
to scheduling conflicts, to just not getting the scripts he
thought worth doing.

But surely one reason had to do with family crises—successive crises, really, in both his real and his professional families.

In the week before he died in June 2013—mind you, this was almost six years after *The Sopranos* had ended—food-writer-turned-*Sopranos*-chronicler Brett Martin published a story in *GQ* magazine that described an epic four-day AWOL Jim went on as the crew was trying to shoot a complicated scene for the 2002 season finale. The scene required a helicopter (the sine qua non of expensive action thrillers) and the rental of the Westchester County Airport. It was a Friday night set, and the crew spent their time switching the schedule to shoot the handful of scenes that didn't require Tony Soprano. But he never showed up.

Missing a big scene was not unheard of. People on *The Sopranos* crew had first gotten used to the sounds of farm animals—chickens, horses, that sort of thing, pigs were rare, though—coming out of Jim's trailer before he did a scene. Animal sounds were part of his warm-up for performing. And everybody knew he could destroy refrigerators and telephone booths, and put his fist through stage-set walls, when he couldn't remember his lines. He'd been late, or gone missing, before.

"His fits were passive-aggressive," Martin wrote. "He would claim to be sick, refuse to leave his Tribeca apartment, or simply not show up. The next day, inevitably, he would feel so wretched about his behavior and the massive logistical disruptions it had caused—akin to turning an aircraft carrier on a dime—that he would treat cast and crew to extravagant gifts. 'All of a sudden there'd be a sushi chef at lunch,' one crew member remembered. 'Or we'd all get massages.' It had come to be understood by all involved as part of the price of doing business, the trade-off for getting the remarkably intense, fully inhabited Tony Soprano that Gandolfini offered."

But this disappearance spooled out into two, three, four days. Scriptwriter Terry Winter told Brett Martin he was so worried that when he heard a radio report while driving to work that began, "Sad news from Hollywood today . . ." he immediately thought Gandolfini was dead.

That proved to be greatly exaggerated. On the fourth day, the production company got a call from Jim, from a beauty salon in Brooklyn, asking someone to send a car to pick him up. He'd walked in with no money and no ID and asked the owner to call the only number he could remember for the offices.

They sent a car.

GQ's timing for this article was uncanny. Combined with the utter shock of Gandolfini's sudden death, it seemed to establish a sort of James Dean-too-reckless-to-live scenario for another uncommonly electric actor. Soap and success may not be as quick as a massacre, but they are just as deadly in the end.

The pressure was intense, of course, but it wasn't en-

tirely coming from the need to prepare for the next pretend murder or apt malapropism. On February 1, 2001,
Gandolfini had left Marcy's duplex in the West Village.
He never went back. A year later, in March 2002, he filed
for divorce.

Going through a New York City divorce while starring in the hottest television show in the country is something shy people should avoid. In the same way the press
would love the stories of *Sopranos* actors getting pinched
for felonies and minor mischief, they adored the idea of
James Gandolfini with marriage troubles. Some papers and
TV gossip shows, naturally enough, led their accounts with
comparisons of Tony's marriage to Carmela with the Gandolfinis' relationship in real life.

For James, it was excruciating. Marcy told friendly out-
lets that she was mystified by his decision, and wondered
darkly about "something bipolar or manic depressive."
Then, in October 2002, *The National Enquirer* published a
story based on a source who claimed to have seen legal
papers prepared for the divorce case. *The Enquirer* wrote
that Marcy claimed Gandolfini had entered drug and alcohol rehabilitation in 1998, and that costars like Julia
Roberts and Edie Falco had both tried to get him to stop
using drugs. It quoted Marcy naming fifty-two people
who were aware of James's drug use, including everyone
from other *Sopranos* actors to Steve Tyler of Aerosmith.

The Enquirer has since taken the story off its Web site,
but an October 17 *Daily News* account summed it up:

Marcy kept a diary that included claims that "Jim would go on a drug binge every 10 to 14 days." . . . He [often] woke up somewhere not knowing his whereabouts. [Marcy] later found out he would do drugs with various bimbos and women and have sex with them.

She also said in her diary that "James would get drunk and make a fist and punch himself repeatedly in the head to see if he could get a reaction from [Marcy] during a quarrel."

Marcy said her husband bought a gun for protection while traveling to Harlem to buy drugs.

Marcy's lawyer, Norman Sheresky, acknowledged that the claims were contained in papers not filed in court, but were "attorney-client correspondence that was private."

Such charges are often the stuff of celebrity divorce. Wudarski later claimed that she was "annoyed" those charges went public, saying she never intended for that to happen. And of course it is an old tabloid tactic to run negative stories unless the star does an on-the-record interview.

And that's what happened, after a special PR consultant was hired to guide the star through this ordeal. Gandolfini, who hated giving interviews, especially about his personal life, sat down with *The National Enquirer* in October 2002, to admit he'd had a problem with cocaine and alcohol four years earlier.

He started out with a criticism of celebrity culture itself, saying, "God, I can't believe I'm doing this. . . . I've watched celebrities doing this. It's like a rite of passage. But I'm clean and sober now. I'm done with everything."

Drugs were part of the nightclub scene where he'd worked in the 1980s, Gandolfini said, and that was where he'd first encountered them. He insisted that it was all over now, that he'd gone to Alcoholics Anonymous from time to time, and that his problems were in his past, from a period before he was an international star and he'd had a son. The Associated Press ran an item, GANDOLFINI ADMITS PAST DRUG ABUSE, on October 17.

Friends and professional associates of Gandolfini's say the experience was harrowing. To get married just as this incredible fame had descended and then divorced as dealing with it became a daily routine was an assault on Gandolfini's dignity like none he'd ever endured. And it left him snakebit as far as the press was concerned for the rest of his life.

Particularly galling was the way the press got hold of intimate details of his personal life by playing sides in the divorce. Jim had never had anything to do with the *New York Post*, the Rupert Murdoch tabloid that thrived on scandalous celebrity stories. (That may have been his mistake—the *Post* can treat celebs well or nastily, but the tone of their coverage is pretty much determined by whether or not the subject gives them access.) Now, Marcy was willing to sit down with *Post* columnist Cindy Adams to say she "always believed Jim would be there for me. That he'd take care of me and love me, as I did him. That we'd be together ninety years.

"I became close to his father, his sisters, Leta and Joanne [sic], his brother-in-law, Eddie," Wudarski continued. "They became my family. He gave me a family and now he's taken them from me. I won't have them anymore because they'll back him, as they should. That's even though his father said to me, 'I know Jim's a handful.' And, 'I'm sorry. This is not the way we raised him.'"

One of Jim's best friends told me that he had always advised Gandolfini to handle the press gently, because anything else wasn't worth it. "I told him it was like he was on guard duty," the friend says, and takes the pose of a soldier stiffly holding a rifle. "Don't slap that mosquito, because you're not supposed to move, and if you slap it the sergeant major will come along and make you dig a six-by-six-foot-deep hole to bury that mosquito in. It's not worth it."

When the case went to court, the celebrity media were disappointed. The settlement was amicable, the press was shut out, and Gandolfini has consistently pointed out how famously he and Michael's mother have gotten on ever since. In December 2002, Gandolfini and Wudarski were divorced. She kept their adjoining condos in the West Village, worth an estimated $2 million, and Michael, then three years old, continued to live with her. James bought a condo downtown in nearby Tribeca, the neighborhood where Robert De Niro lived.

And then, of course, art imitated life. *The Sopranos* being what it was, the 2004 season opened with Tony in the middle of an angry separation from Carmela, which would become one of the main plot lines for the rest of the season.

"Having gone through something similar personally, [it] was a little difficult to have to dredge those things up sometimes," Gandolfini later told a local Florida reporter. "In terms of acting, anything that's huge [personally] just makes you dig real deep.

"It's going to just take you to places that you haven't been before. Sometimes it was hard. It was very difficult some of those days to do some of those things and to continue on into it."

Writers for *The Sopranos*, like everyone else on the set, knew what Gandolfini had been through. They gave Tony lines—"I'm old-school. I don't believe in this separation . . . and divorce," he screams at Carmela—that didn't take much imagination to assume echoed the actor's own feelings. Unlike Jim, however, Tony went straight to coercion, threatening to end Carmela's nice suburban lifestyle and personal security. "He's got a lot of rage," Gandolfini said.

Aston told me that Gandolfini usually called writers "vampires," because they'd listen to you sympathetically, like any friend, and then turn around and use what you'd told them in a scene. It was the *Post* that made the meanest play on this game of real and false, quoting Marcy saying you could tell Jim wasn't Tony Soprano because "Tony would never hurt his family."

———

When an actual family fights about money, they're usually really fighting about love. But when a theater family fights about money, it's about money—and love, too, just not for each other, but for the audience.

In 2003 the cast of *The Sopranos* started a fight about money that threatened, for a time, to end the show. When it was over, it turned out all along to have been about the audience for *The Sopranos*, which happened to be the most multiplatform-accessible hit TV show in history. They were a different kind of audience for a different kind of show, and they suggested new possibilities for entertainment that aspired to art.

It started when four of the show regulars banded together—an idea inspired by four regular players on *The West Wing*, who had recently done the same thing with great success—to demand more money per episode. Jamie-Lynn Sigler (Tony's daughter, Meadow), Robert Iler (his son, A.J.), Drea de Matteo (Christopher's girlfriend Adriana), and Tony Sirico (Paulie Walnuts) were all getting $20,000 to $30,000 per episode, and they wanted an increase to $100,000. That would add up to $1.3 million for each per year—maybe not Kelsey Grammar money, but more than the dog got on *Frasier*.

The West Wing quartet had more than doubled their per episode salaries to over $70,000 after missing a couple of early read-throughs, so the demands weren't beyond reason. Even more troubling to HBO executives, however, were press reports that they weren't facing just the Four

Horsemen in supporting roles. Lead actor James Gandolfini was waiting to hear how their negotiations went before he decided to set an asking price of his own for the next season.

This smelled terribly of unionization, employees banding together to demand higher wages—something that had not been happening much in America for some time in 2003. The year before, at the behest of Steve Buscemi, who would both perform as an actor and direct some of *The Sopranos'* best-known episodes, Gandolfini had made radio ads for the New York City Uniformed Fireman's Association in their contract dispute with the city. Buscemi used to be a fireman himself. The suits at HBO worried that they might be cast in the same light as city union-busters. It left hurt feelings, and the dispute became public very fast.

HBO said publicly that Gandolfini was being "greedy," that he was more interested in his own ability to earn big money than in the rest of the crew. At one point HBO shut down production for a week, throwing all the grips and caterers and cameramen out of work with no pay, blaming the show's star for it in the press. Gandolfini filed suit to dissolve his own two-year $10 million contract. HBO felt it had no choice but nip this sort of thing in the bud, and it responded with a $100 million lawsuit of its own against Gandolfini, charging him with trying to break a legitimate contract and destroy what together they'd made into a very lucrative property.

Jim tried several personal overtures to calm the waters, one at the Screen Actors Guild awards ceremony in March, walking over to the gathered HBO execs and telling them how much he "appreciated" what the company had done for him, and again at a private meeting later in that week. The response every time was pretty stony. Producer Brad Grey—who had noted that contract negotiations at *The Sopranos* had started sounding like a Mafia shakedown— did a last-minute negotiation that found a compromise.

Gandolfini's salary was more than doubled again, to over $800,000 per episode; all told, he stood to earn more than $13 million for the fifth season, more than the $11 million HBO had first offered, but less than the $16 million he'd initially demanded. The rest of the cast and crew went back to work immediately, with back pay for the week they'd missed. That meant a lot to Gandolfini at the closing.

And the four regular players who'd started the whole thing? Their salaries more than doubled too, to around $75,000 per episode.

But the story doesn't end there. After the brinkmanship of the 2003 salary negotiations, things were quiet on the money question for two years. But only a very few people knew that some of that quiet had been bought by Jim personally.

"He was a really good guy," actor Steve Schirripa, who played Uncle Junior's right hand, Bobby "Bacala" Baccalieri, told New York's WFAN radio station after Gandolfini died. "A really good guy. As good of an actor as he was, he was a better guy. A generous guy. The guy gave us $33,000 each—sixteen people. There's a lot of people who made a lot more money than him. In season four he called every one of the cast members and gave us a check. He said, 'Thanks for sticking by me.' It's like buying sixteen people a car."

The other way of looking at it is $528,000 out of Gandolfini's $13 million for the fifth season went to his fellow *Sopranos* cast members. While it's probably true that other actors have done extremely generous things with the money they've received, stories like this one have few if any contemporary precedents. Certainly not at that amount. And it goes a long way toward explaining the loyalty—extending to their own sort of *omerta* about James's personal life and his behavior on the set—that his cast mates and friends consistently express for James.

It definitely set a tone on the set—the play was the thing, not the ego of the individual actors. Aston told Gandolfini in those years that he'd be able to work as an actor as long as he wanted to, for the rest of his life, after *The Sopranos*. But he knew some of his fellow actors weren't so lucky. And it was the ensemble that made it work, that gave them all the best career opportunity they'd ever likely have.

The 2003 negotiations happened when the revolutionary

impact of *The Sopranos* was only just beginning to be understood. Nobody thought a show like it could ever be syndicated on basic cable (it was, in an expurgated version—the actors really didn't say "fuck" as much as everyone thought—earning an initial $195 million from A&E less than two years later). All the books, DVDs, video games, spin-off merchandise, and promotional publicity HBO got from its signature series were only beginning to be totaled up.

And, more important, the negotiations acknowledged something fundamental about American cultural habits in the new century. Movies were once group cultural events, part of a night out on the town, done in public in the great gathering places like downtown movie palaces and suburban cineplexes. And those places are dying.

Actually, public space in the United States has been defunded and marginalized since the early 1980s, and by the turn of the century we were only beginning to understand the impact of those policies. But one effect was declining movie ticket sales and the explosion of big, flat-screen TVs in living rooms around the country. The "theater crowd" was becoming virtual. Cable TV was a new medium that had different ways of finding an audience for serious art—it could conjure that paying audience out of the living rooms into which they'd retreated. Soon they'd be able to watch *The Sopranos* in an eighty-six-hour marathon on DVD, or on TiVo, or any other on-demand service, and while the producers made money off those forms, they didn't show up in TV ratings or audience share stats.

The sour blossom that David Chase had fashioned out of frustration for his native state, which James Gandolfini helped turn into a vehicle for sympathy and pathos, had found a huge audience out there. Because the world really was filled with simulated New Jerseys: Everywhere you had a corporate back-office securing profits by shaving labor costs and dodging regulations, whether in the United Kingdom or Fujian province or the suburbs of Sydney, you had a little piece of Jersey. Really, they were everywhere you looked.

As Tony said in the first episode, "It's good to get in on something on the ground floor." And in the matter of finding a new audience, *The Sopranos* did not come too late.

Even though he compromised for his crew at the very end, the 2003 negotiations were a personal triumph for James Gandolfini. Tony had been helpless to save his wild ducks, but Jim saved his, and gave them a nice raise to boot. At least, all the wild ducks in his professional family.

In four years, Gandolfini had leaped from working class to the 1 percent, but he had not forgotten where he'd come from, or all the people he was constantly thanking for his own success. "All the fuss during *The Sopranos* really was pretty ridiculous," he said much later. "None of us expected it to last, and it lasted almost ten years.

Dan Bischoff

Honestly? I don't think I'm that different. I've lived in the same apartment for years. I've kept a lot of the same friends. I'm still grumpy and miserable. . . . But in a good way!"

8.

The Pressures of Success (2003–2007)

Once, when *The Sopranos* was in full swing, Jim Gandolfini found himself passing someone in a doorway only to see the other man's face go white with fear. Befuddled, he went on inside, and then it hit him: "Oh, he thinks I'm Tony."

It's one thing if an actor becomes famous playing Superman, say, or maybe a wizard, or a space explorer. But if your character is a kind of masquerade, like the don of the New Jersey mob, which exists right now, this afternoon, just across the river from a really big city that everybody knows is actually here, it can live with you like it lives in the minds of its fans. The fans can be rich and important people, but the alienation is the same.

"When people want to ask you to dinner sometimes and they don't know you," Jim told *GQ*'s Chris Heath in 2004, "they want Tony Soprano to come to dinner. They don't want Jim Gandolfini to come to dinner. I would bore the fucking tits off them."

Method actors have a long history of consternation over their talent, particularly as they grow older. Marlon Brando was famously contemptuous of the profession he had mastered and changed so fundamentally: His movie sets had to be plastered with dozens of giant cue cards just out of sightline of the cameras because he found memorization such a drag. Some actors think the whole thing is a fluke, a vacation from their real job. Robert Mitchum (who was working as a machinist when he started looking for acting parts) once stumped a BBC interviewer who was gushing over his professional achievement by interrupting to say, "Look, I have two kinds of acting. One on a horse and one off a horse. That's it."

Lee Marvin perhaps said it best: "You spend the first forty years of your life trying to get in this business, and the next forty years trying to get out. And then, when you're making the bread, who needs it?"

It is, as Roger Bart says, all just "make-believe," and sometimes a man wants to be real. Or he wants this thing that he does, that captivates so many people, to break down the fourth wall and become something as real as real. Asked by Heath why he became an actor, Jim said this:

"To maybe vomit my emotions out of me," he says, an answer both flip and serious. He smiles. "Am I making this hard for you?" he asks. And he offers a more considered reply: "I think I feel a lot. I never wanted to do

*business or anything. People interest me, and the way
things affect them. And I also have a big healthy affinity for the middle class and the blue-collar, and I don't
like the way they're treated, and I don't like the way the
government is treating them now. I have a good healthy
dose of anger about all of that. And I think that if I kept
it in, it wouldn't have been very good. I would have
been fired a lot. So I found this silly way of living that
allows me to occasionally stand up for them a little bit.
And mostly make some good money and act like a silly
fool."*

*Gandolfini—who will vote for John Kerry in
November—offers examples: health care, the removal of
sports from many Oregon schools, corporate tax avoid-
ance. "The money that goes to these islands offshore!" he
exclaims. "I paid more taxes than Enron one year—
what the fuck is that about?"*

What indeed? The kind of success he'd had was almost
unimaginable—although, truth be told, he *did* imagine it,
back when he was thinking of creating a stage persona
named Jimmy Leather, and tried to warn his mom and
dad and two sisters that his fame might get to be "a pain
in the ass." It just took so long maybe he'd forgotten about
it. He certainly lived his life as if he had just kept doing
his work as dutifully as he could and then fame happened,
like a pile of old newspapers falling on a hoarder.

"He charmed a lot of people in the industry with that 'humble craftsman' thing," says his Meisner technique teacher, Kathryn Gately. It played into another perception of Jim, that he was "grounded," that he had no starry-eyed illusions about a life in the theater.

Some of this is what being "a regular Jersey guy," as everybody called him all his life, means. But Gandolfini had a special quality of "regularness." In almost every job he ever had he seemed to effortlessly attract attention from the boss—whether the job was delivering soda water for Gimme Seltzer or managing Private Eyes' bouncers or playing a slightly jaded, philosophically inclined hitman in *True Romance* for director Tony Scott.

And bosses—not just Hollywood directors, but bosses—liked him. Not always, of course, because Jim could be difficult, moody, and demanding. But generally, they accepted him for what he was.

If that seems at odds with his union-loving, working-class-sympathizing affect, well, you think about class as if it were all about money and never about values. Take, for example, what Jim told Heath about his father and privilege, one of his most-cited quotes at the time of his funeral:

Gandolfini seems suspicious of the position that The Sopranos' *success has put him in. The topic of his own celebrity is one that makes him nervous. He doesn't want to seem ungrateful. "I find fame ugly," he says. "My*

Above: Jamie Gandolfini with his dad, James John Gandolfini, in Park Ridge when he was about three years old. (*Santa Gandolfini*)

Right: "Fini" at Park Ridge High, with his perfect "David Cassidy" head of hair. (*Courtesy of Park Ridge High School*)

Above: Gandolfini, with fellow senior Yvie Campbell, voted "Best Looking" in the 1980 Park Ridge High yearbook. (*Courtesy of Park Ridge High School*)

Above: That same year he was also voted "Biggest Flirt"—and the yearbook staff found the perfect illustration. (*Courtesy of Park Ridge High School*)

Local girl dies in crash

CALDWELL — A 22-year old West Caldwell woman was killed instantly in an accident early Sunday morning when the car she was driving crossed Bloomfield Avenue, wrapped around a utility pole and broke in half just behind the driver's seat. The front portion of the vehicle crashed into a store at 190 Bloomfield Avenue.

Police said that the dead woman, Lynn Marie Jacobson, was evidently driving west at a high speed on Bloomfield Avenue when she lost control of the vehicle, crossed the avenue and collided with the pole and the store. Police said she died instantly and the coroner's report listed multiple fractures of the head as the cause of death.

There was no evidence of the cause of the accident in the vehicle, police said, and declined to speculate on possibilities.

Miss Jacobson was employed as a hostess at The Manor, Prospect Avenue, West Orange, and it was theorized that she was returning home from work when the accident occurred at 4:45 a.m.

The crash occurred at the bend of Bloomfield Avenue as it enters Caldwell, near the former Erie Railroad Station. The car, a 1971 Ford Mustang, was towed from the scene.

Miss Jacobson, daughter of John and Alyson Jacobson, was employed by the Media Management Public Relations and Advertising Co., New York City. She had worked at The Manor as a hostess for about three years.

Lynn Jacobson

A 1977 graduate of James Caldwell High School, Miss Jacobson received a bachelor of arts degree in communication from Rutgers University, New Brunswick in May, 1981. Born in Pittsburgh, Pa., she lived most of her life in West Caldwell. She was active in St. Peter's Episcopal Church, Essex Fells and had also been a volunteer for the March of Dimes campaign in the area.

During her years at Rutgers she was a member of the Student Welcoming Committee.

In addition to her parents, Miss Jacobson is survived by her twin sister, Leslie Ann, another sister, Gail, both of West Caldwell and her maternal grandparents, Mr. and Mrs. H.C. Bourne of Ohio.

The funeral was held yesterday in St. Peter's Episcopal Church, Essex Fells, with the Rev. Dr. David St. George officiating. Interment was in Restland Memorial Park, East Hanover.

In lieu of flowers, contributions were requested to the West Essex Chapter of the March of Dimes or to the St. Peter's Church Memorial Fund.

FATAL CRASH — Lynn Jacobson, 22 of West Caldwell, was killed early Sunday morning when the car shown above veered from the westbound lane of Bloomfield Avenue, smashed into a utility pole just east of 180 Bloomfield and broke in half. The front half of the vehicle smashed into a store front at 190 Bloomfield Ave. Miss Jacobson was killed instantly, police said. (Gene Collerd photo)

Above: Lynn Jacobson's obituary from *The Progressive*, the local paper for the Caldwells; Jacobson's dark blue Mustang was split in two by a concrete utility pole. Gandolfini credited her with making him want to be an actor in his acceptance speech for his third Emmy in 2003.

TARANTULAS DANCING

SUSAN ASTON
(212) 724-1110

JAMES GANDOLFINI
(212) 874-5300

Above: James Gandolfini's first actor's headshot, ca. 1985.
(*Courtesy of Mike Wills*)
Left: Back cover for the playbill for *Tarantulas Dancing*, ca, 1985.
The play helped both actors land roles in the Broadway production
of *A Streetcar Named Desire*, starring Alec Baldwin and Jessica Lange.
(*Courtesy of Mike Wills*)

Above: Gandolfini on location in Long Branch, New Jersey, for *The Sopranos*, joking with police officers, in April 2007. The wind off the ocean was freezing. (*Mark Dye*/The Star-Ledger)

Above: Gandolfini signs autographs in Long Branch. He'd sign anything that came to hand, even dollar bills. By the middle of the first season, he was the biggest celebrity in his home state. (*Mark Dye*/The Star-Ledger)

Above: Gandolfini with his first wife, Marcy Wudarski, and their son, Michael, dressed as a gangster for the Children Affected by AIDS Foundation's Dream Halloween party at Roseland in New York City in October 2007. (*Theo Wargo, ImageWire/Getty Images*)

Above: Gandolfini with high school drama teacher Ann Comarato (left) and former student director Donna Mancinelli, at a fundraiser for the OctoberWoman Foundation for Breast Cancer Research in Park Ridge, when *The Sopranos* was at its height. Mancinelli's family had shared the Gandolfinis' summer house in Lavallette on the Jersey Shore when they were kids, and she got him to bring the cast down for OctoberWoman several years in a row. "Fini" thanked Comarato in her high school yearbook, writing, "I'm a pain in the ass and I need someone to keep my but [sic] in line. Thanks.... When I'm a rich actor (sure) I'll come visit you." (*Courtesy of Ann Comarato*)

Above: Lora Somoza and Gandolfini on the red carpet for the fifth season premiere of *The Sopranos* at Radio City Music Hall in Manhattan, 2004. (*James Devaney, WireImage/Getty Images*)

Above: Gandolfini outside Holsten's ice cream parlor in Bloomfield on March 22, 2007, to shoot the ending of *The Sopranos*. (*Tony Kurdzuk/*The Star-Ledger*)

Above: Tony Sirico and Gandolfini with two U.S. warrant officers and Joe Stinchcomb, former tackle for the Superbowl-winning New Orleans Saints, in Afghanistan. Sirico, himself a veteran, helped get Gandolfini involved with Wounded Warriors, the charity that helps severely wounded soldiers readjust to civilian life. (*Mike Sullivan*)

Above: The Sopranos crew addresses a tent full of soldiers at Bagram Air Base in Afghanistan; President Barack Obama was in a tent next door, but that didn't reduce the crowd of fans (*Sopranos* DVDs were a hot item overseas). (*Mike Sullivan*)

Above: Deborah Lin Gandolfini, James, his son Michael, and Marcy Wudarski at the 2008 Dream Halloween party for the Children Affected by AIDS Foundation, at Roseland. (*Shawn Ehlers for Children Affected by AIDS Foundation, WireImage/Getty Images*)

Above: James Gandolfini posing with his two sisters, Johanna (left) and Leta, at his wedding to Deborah Lin in Hawaii, August 30, 2008. (*Courtesy of Tom Richardson*)

father always said a million times, 'We're peasants.' His concept of life was, 'No one's better than anybody else.' And, 'The rich are thieves,' pretty much. To find yourself being treated in a different bit of status, even in the small amount that I have compared to Brad Pitt or . . . it's just a little odd for me, to get that slightly different treatment sometimes. And I'm uncomfortable with it."

Does it feel like you've betrayed your natural team, the peasants?

"I want nothing to do with privilege. That's basically what it is. I don't like privilege. That's all I'm saying. Take that as you want."

Spoken like a true citizen of Park Ridge. But, as an expression of ideology, it's very rooted in Old Worldliness. Peasants? In America? Well, in New Jersey?

Actually, you put it that way, maybe it does make some sense. Maybe growing up Italian-American west of the Hudson, Gandolfini saw a world of peasants and nobs. Members of both classes had different responsibilities. You measure the person by how well he or she played their role. You could be a good worker or a bad manager, or vice versa. He himself was a guy who took pride in his work and tried to do a good job, and doing it well was much more important than his own feelings.

You can easily underestimate just how appealing that attitude is in an often unpredictable industry. It's like the time the twenty-four-year-old Brando went up to Provincetown to audition for Stanley Kowalski in *A Streetcar Named Desire*. Brando did a reading for Tennessee Williams, and then hung around for a couple of days to do some badly needed house repairs.

He got the part.

And Jim understood that everybody is flawed. Hamlet said, "Use every man after his deserts, and who shall 'scape whipping?" Close friends of Gandolfini's in Hollywood told me that Jim could not warm to anyone who seemed too perfect. But confess to him some overpowering weakness—for anything—and he was loyal. The deal was the same as it was with the Rutgers crew: we'll always be there for each other.

It's almost a character actor's approach to life: find the flaw that explicates the character, then understand him. Once you do that, you can love him, and make everybody else love him, too. That's what Gandolfini did with Eddy in *The Juror,* and Winston Baldry in *The Mexican*. With Tony perhaps most of all.

Being a great character actor doesn't reward going it alone or developing grand theories of human nature. It's *about* observing others to understand them, and seeing the fullness of their character in relationship to their society. T. J. Foderaro says Jim could fix you with a look across a crowded room that implied life was crazy, but you and he knew it. There was something a touch fatalistic about that attitude—it isn't in our power to make the world less crazy: We can just make it a little better for those we care about by letting them know they're not alone.

I haven't come across a single person involved in the production of *The Sopranos* who doesn't think it was a wonderful experience, a once-in-a-lifetime opportunity for actors, writers, directors, PR folks, agents, producers—everybody is misty-eyed about being part of the art project that was that show. Toward the end, Edie Falco told *Vanity Fair* about moving on as an actress (before her opportunity for *Nurse Jackie* came along), looking at possible scripts, and just being horrified—"It's all terrible. It's scary."

Everyone, that is, except Jim Gandolfini and David Chase.

Chase, of course, is a pessimist's pessimist—if something is going well, it's probably a trap. When he admits that he was very lucky to have *The Sopranos* turn out so well, he almost makes it seem grudging, like it was a fluke. What would you expect from someone raised in downtown Newark's Little Italy whose mom once threatened to put out his eye with a fork if he asked for a Hammond organ? Good things are not for this person.

But for Gandolfini, there was the pressure to perform, over and over. He had his tricks—the pointy stone in his shoe, staying up two nights in a row, whatever's best for conveying anger. But those things are like drugs, they wear off, or demand greater intensities for the same effect. And as everyone tells you they love what you do, and strangers stop you on the street calling out your character's name, and you have more money than you ever expected to earn, well, some of those emotions become harder to summon, especially violent anger.

"I worried about the toll playing Tony took," says Kathryn Gately, who watched *The Sopranos* from the very beginning and was thrilled by her former student's riveting performance. "I saw the weight gain. You could almost feel the stress."

The stress was sort of the point. In his few interviews, Jim would often deride questions about how he was adjusting to success as "princess problems," far less meaningful than the problems of real people in the real world. There was all that money, after all. He didn't want to seem "ungrateful."

But people loved seeing a semipowerful character (Tony was always enmeshed in a pecking order, like any corporate goon) barely control his frustration and anger. They could sympathize. Portraying Tony started to become a personal reversal, a daily journey into a world of perilous doubt and fear that was the opposite of his real life. The conflict was symbolized physically by his circumstances, going each day from his West Village apartment or, later, his horse country colonial or Tribeca condo, across the Queensboro Bridge to the old bread factory by the off-ramp that housed Silvercup Studios and *The Sopranos* sets. There, amid crumbling walls, plastic folding chairs, and wastebaskets full of used Styrofoam cups (we won't try to number the mice population) were perfect reproductions of Tony's West Caldwell manse in all its beige spotlessness. The actors themselves—and the writers, too—hung out all day in rooms that made an inner city hospital look like a five-star hotel.

It was his breakthrough role and it was hard, emotionally grinding work. Not to mention, it made some people go white when they saw him coming.

Gandolfini came to want more than anything, like other TV stars before him, to live down the role that made millions of Americans believe they knew him like they knew their brother-in-law. Tony wasn't him, and he could do so much more.

He'd always been a fan of *The Honeymooners*—"I can't tell you how much I heard that 'To the moon!' thing," Aston says—but as *The Sopranos* matured and his fame grew, Gandolfini began to study the career of Jackie Gleason. Jim wanted to do more comedy, for one thing. He liked, he said, "stupid comedies" that the uninitiated might think beneath his skill level.

But there were limits: He was offered the part of Don Lino, the godfather shark in DreamWorks' *Shark Tale,* a 2004 hit, but turned it down because it was too much like a parody of *The Sopranos*. (Michael Imperioli took the part of Frankie, the mob hit-shark, and Don Lino was voiced by Robert De Niro who, after *Analyze This* and *That*, had no qualms about sending up his career as a mobster.) Gandolfini was offered Curly in the *Three Stooges* remake, and wanted to do it, too, but never thought the script was good enough. (Showbiz body-type irony: Will Sasso, who ultimately played Curly in the 2012 *Three Stooges* revival, had himself done an absolutely dead-on parody of Tony Soprano on *MADtv*—he made himself look more like Gandolfini than he did Curly, which is saying something.)

Gleason was more than just another fat comic. He was a talent maker, for one thing, able to use his place in show business to help others, like Art Carney as Norton, or Frank Fontaine as Crazy Guggenheim, make a name for themselves. He always seemed rooted to a particular place, too—his native Brooklyn at first, then Broadway, and finally Miami Beach—not unlike Jim the Jersey Guy. Gleason had his serious side, and did a number of movies with claims to deep angst (*Gigot*, anyone?), but he was beloved as an ensemble comedian, and especially for his bus driver protagonist Ralph Kramden from *The Honeymooners*. Most of Gleason's characters gave voice to common men, but Ralph was an icon.

On break from *The Sopranos* in 2004, Gandolfini took on his first really Gleasonesque role, Nick Murder in *Romance & Cigarettes*, written and directed by actor John Turturro. *Romance & Cigarettes* was orphaned by a Hollywood merger and only got limited distribution in the United States in 2005. It has an all-star cast, with Susan Sarandon playing Gandolfini's wife, Kate Winslet as his mistress, and Aida Turturro, Elaine Stritch, Eddie Izzard, Christopher Walken, and Steve Buscemi all doing memorable cameos. It's a kind of opera based on Top-40 pop songs, which the characters lip-sync and then take over as their own, belting their hearts out from a cul-de-sac tract house in Queens near the JFK airport. Walken's version of the Tom Jones hit "Delilah" is usually thought to be the best set piece.

Gandolfini played an Italian-American ironworker, tempted to leave his family for a younger woman, who is surprised to learn he's got terminal cancer. He does suburban ballets with a chorus of garbagemen, a telephone repairman, a welder, and later cops and firemen. Every male, from six to sixty, in this middle-class neighborhood of vinyl-sided single-family homes joins him in Engelbert Humperdinck's "Lonely Is a Man Without Love" as they roll through their daily routines. It's absolutely zany, a bit undisciplined as a film, but Gandolfini shows a comfort with the material and his own physicality that promises a great deal. His willingness to do things other actors might find humiliating—like producing a long, excruciating fart before he collapses—is fantastic. The dance numbers are often hilarious. Plus, he sings, rather well, and wears a pencil mustache for half the film.

Turturro said he wanted Gandolfini for the role because

no other actor had "the heart" it needed. But whatever hopes James had that *Romance & Cigarettes* would send Tony to sleep with the fishes were disappointed—though Walken's version of "Delilah" became a minor YouTube sensation, the movie itself made little impact. As the final season of *The Sopranos* approached, he was still Tony to everyone.

At least from the outside, *The Sopranos* professional family was a happy family by 2004, and all happy families are alike. Gandolfini's personal life in those years was, if not unhappy, at the very least happy in its own way.

Gandolfini had met Lora Somoza in the production offices of *The Mexican* back in 2000, just before shooting started, on the day he dropped by to try to quit. Director Gore Verbinski was out, and Somoza, who was working as his assistant, wound up on the receiving end of James's self-doubt. He couldn't get the part, was he really right for it, there were other guys who could do it better; she listened sympathetically while trying, as calmly as she could, to get Verbinkski on the phone to ask what to do.

By the time Verbinkski caught up with Lora, her job had become keeping the star of *The Sopranos* in the picture.

Over the next couple of years, Gandolfini and Somoza were photographed together frequently, in New York and

170

Los Angeles, as a couple. By the time of his divorce in 2002, he told the *Daily Mail* that she was his date to industry premieres and awards ceremonies. Somoza, who was born in 1973, says Jim always called her "Fatty"—she's quite slender—and he used to say that standing together, they looked like the "number ten." Somoza has dark eyes and full lips, and tends to favor an unaffected, natural look most of the time. In 2004, he proposed, and they were officially engaged for two years.

Like Marcy, Somoza was from a working-class family, but hers had immigrant roots, too—her father was Mexican. She brought out his childlike qualities—Somoza told the *Daily Mail* tabloid that Jim "was always a smart-ass, playing practical jokes and doing silly things in order to embarrass me. He would sing silly songs and goof around."

Somoza was with Gandolfini when *The Sopranos* was at the height of its popularity and his celebrity as an actor at its brightest. When she met him, he had already become, much to his amazement, an American sex symbol in his early forties.

The year the couple got engaged, Chris Heath asked how he was enjoying his enduring status as one of the sexiest men alive.

"There is no enduring status," Jim answered. "I have no answer to any of that, and I don't see it in my life. I think I play a character that likes to fuck and happens to fuck a lot on the show, and that might be something people enjoy, but other than that . . . I mean, the guy has a healthy libido. That's about all that's healthy about him. I don't have anything to say about that. It's flattering that anybody could—at a certain age and a certain paunch and a certain baldness—the fact that anyone would suppose their attention on you is extremely flattering."

This was the sort of question he didn't like to answer—you can tell when he starts stumbling his words at the end. Gandolfini refused to do on-camera interviews about himself or his series all through its run (at the very end, he did an appearance on *Charlie Rose,* but that was with all sixteen regular cast members, and a couple of years later he did *Inside the Actors Studio* with James Lipton, for the students and for Susan Aston, who teaches there, but that was about it). He gave a handful of print interviews (Chris Heath's was the best) from time to time, but he usually avoided personal questions in those.

He told his staff in Hollywood that he wanted the audience to focus on the character of Tony Soprano, not him, so media appearances were a distraction. But then, after *The Sopranos* had become show business legend, it became an excuse. He'd never done interviews during *The Sopranos*—what about his latest project or his personal life now merited a public discussion if the most revolutionary TV show of all time did not?

A good question, but Somoza believed it went deeper than that. She did not think James enjoyed fame, not only because he was shy but because fans often left him nonplussed (like the guy who pulled up his shirt to show Jim that he had Tony's face—really, Gandolfini's face—tattooed all over his back). Seeing Jim as a "sex symbol," like his friend Brad Pitt, was similarly ridiculous. He was a regular guy doing his job, like his dad before him.

He couldn't help it if being recognized on the street was the definition of success in this business he had chosen. That is why actors get paid so very well, by the way, whenever they do—because people know who they are and want to see them perform again.

The kind of actor Jim had always wanted to be was the kind that took the role seriously, the kind that sought truth in the performance, not the performer. Somoza said that the pressure of playing Tony Soprano was constant. He would "be" Tony from the moment he went out the door in the morning, throughout a twelve- to sixteen-hour day, and then come home with seven pages of Tony's dialogue to memorize.

Asked directly if she thought the pressure drove him to drink and use drugs, Somoza would only say she'd be surprised if anyone keeping such a schedule didn't seek relief somehow. And the story of his four-day disappearance from the set in 2002 confirms what he told *The National Enquirer* years later, that his claims of being "clean and sober" since 1998 were, well, exaggerated. He admitted that his drinking and cocaine use got worse during his marriage.

It's not much of a news flash: CREATIVE ARTISTS LIKE

TO GET INEBRIATED. Actually, that's a fair headline for most professions. But because some artists have laid claim to a special dispensation, there is a subgenre of artist biographies that focuses on substance abuse. John Cassavetes's script for *She's So Lovely*, in which Gandolfini played the heel back in 1997, would fit in such a story, since it's a long paean to the beauties in the bottle.

Jim had enough of a problem that he went to Alcoholics Anonymous now and again, though he never really was consistent in his attendance. After one of the early seasons of *The Sopranos* wrapped he went off to a farmhouse-style rehab center in upstate New York. In 2009 he acknowledged he'd had problems since that first *Enquirer* interview, but insisted he was clean once more. What we know for sure is that Gandolfini functioned as an artist throughout—that same year, he went back to Broadway, as one of four actors in *The God of Carnage*, to rave reviews.

Jim and Lora never set a date. "Sometimes love does not conquer all," Somoza told a British tabloid about their breakup. "Sometimes you really want something but life gets in the way and it doesn't happen.

"There was no animosity, no acrimony," Somoza continued. "In fact, my grandmother eventually died from Alzheimer's and Jim knew how much the Alzheimer's Association meant to me and he lent his name, and face, to the Forget-Me-Not Ball—a big fund-raiser" for the charity.

In 2005 his father, James John Gandolfini, died; he'd

been in assisted living for some time. Somoza's grand-mother began suffering from Alzheimer's disease around the same time, and Somoza left New York to care for her back in California. Jim and Somoza never really got back together after that.

Several years after they broke up, Somoza became a sex therapist and Huffington Post blogger—she calls her-self "the naughty Dear Abby"—and she's been hosting the podcast *Between the Sheets with Lora Somoza* in California since 2010. She offers relationship advice and sex tips in a friendly, but very West Coast–oversharing way. At his death, she memorialized Gandolfini in an episode of her show, promoted on her Web site as "a split personality show: We've got the worst book on 'how to get you laid,' foot orgasms you may or may not want, and my special good-bye to my dear friend Jim Gandolfini."

They remained friends, and talked even as recently as a few weeks before his trip to Rome. Somoza said she learned of Jim's death through a phone call from the *New York Post*. She attended Gandolfini's funeral service at Saint John the Divine in New York City, sitting with friends and family.

Before *The Sopranos* ended in 2007, Gandolfini did two more films, both period pieces that cast him, if not as a mobster, as a tough guy. He played Tiny Duffy, a political bagman in Depression-era Louisiana, in *All the King's*

Men, starring Sean Penn and Jude Law (released in 2006, it had originally been scheduled for 2005, and was shot earlier). It's the Huey Long story, this time told in a way closer to Robert Penn Warren's novel than the 1949 version with Broderick Crawford. Although Gandolfini deployed another intermittent southern accent, you couldn't help wishing he'd been cast in the Crawford-Penn role. The scene in which Willie Stark, who's only just learned he's being used to split the vote, stands up to Tiny Duffy in front of a crowd of dirt farmers lets Jim do a very funny deflated blowhard. Gandolfini certainly looked the part more than Penn, and Willie Stark could have used some of Jim's roguish charm. For all its good intentions and professional pedigree, the movie was a critical and box office failure.

In *Lonely Hearts* (2006) he played police detective Charles Hildebrandt, partner to Elmer C. Robinson, played by John Travolta, on the trail of psychotic murderers Martha Beck and Raymond Fernandez, played by Salma Hayek and Jared Leto. Gandolfini tells the story in the voiceover, but it's a drab little tale, as sepia-tinted as the cinematographer's tonal palette, based on a true story that's been made into a movie more than once before. Oddly enough, its ending is similar to that of *The Man Who Wasn't There*, with a smoking electric chair of roughly the same vintage, and the same creepy bondage-mask grace note.

As the final, 2006 season of *The Sopranos* approached, Jim was still Tony. Just when he thought he was out, they pulled him back in.

After two years of salary peace, the actors recognized an opportunity to renegotiate their contracts. HBO had decided to redefine the word "season." Instead of thirteen one-hour-long episodes, they would make twenty, and show them in two "mini-seasons" of twelve and eight episodes each, separated by several months. It was like getting two seasons for one, the actors felt—though in fact, what the network was getting was two-thirds of a season in extra episodes.

Sirico and Van Zandt immediately demanded $200,000 per episode for the extra six; HBO said it was reluctant to go over $90,000 (the two actors were getting $85,000 and $80,000 per, respectively, for the first twelve). The rest of the cast began to demand renegotiations, too. As things began to go public, Gandolfini called a meeting in his apartment in Tribeca to smooth things over.

Season six would consist of twelve episodes that would start airing in November 2006, and nine more episodes that would begin to air in October 2007. HBO agreed to double Sirico's and Van Zandt's salaries, and made similar deals with the thirteen other regular actors. Smaller parts got comparable boosts.

Gandolfini had already settled on a contract: he would make $1 million an episode for the last half season—that is, $9 million, however you want to count your seasons. He was part of the one percent. He'd crossed the river, and for good.

At the New York City premiere of the second part of

the sixth season in October 2007, the last premiere *The Sopranos* would ever have, James Gandolfini walked the red carpet with a pretty former model and actress from Hawaii named Deborah Lin.

9.

After T

"Who am I?" is always a great question, but for actors it's a tease, a commercial challenge, and a personal problem all at once. Especially if you are a famous actor, like the forty-seven-year-old James Gandolfini was in 2008, the first year in almost a decade when he would not be playing Tony Soprano.

In 2001, *Rolling Stone* asked Gandolfini whether his reluctance to talk about himself in public reflected his desire to live an unexamined life, if he preferred to just "get on with things" rather than talk about them—you know, like Tony. But he said he thought of himself as more like another iconic figure.

"Yes, I would do that," he replied initially. "But only because I'm a neurotic mess. I'm really basically just like a 260-pound Woody Allen. . . . There are some days when you say, 'Oh, fuck it,' and some days when I think way too much. As does everybody. I'm no different than anybody else. But you know what? Unless you have some deep

179

problem, I don't know. . . ." He stops himself. "You know what, I shouldn't be talking about therapy. I don't know a thing about it."

Well, he had to know a little about it—at least, about pretend therapy, because that's what he and Lorraine Bracco had been doing then for two years on the set. There had to be a few places where they scratched the overlaps between Tony and Jim. Even mooning her during her reaction shots had to have some kind of therapeutic meaning.

His fame gave him much more leeway to pick and choose the roles he would take and ultimately his onstage identity, the sort of power you work long years in the business to develop. He was in control, but only up to a point. He still could not change his "type," though he could play against it; he could not easily appeal across generational divides, though he could try.

Many people would have taken a vacation after nine years as the most intense antihero in TV history—not a month at the Jersey Shore, but some sort of getaway reward for all the hard work. Jim rented a bigger beach house, but he didn't exactly go on vacation. Although, after *All the King's Men* came out in 2006 and *The Sopranos* wrapped the next year, Gandolfini didn't appear in any films for a couple of years, he didn't really take a break. What he did was start the effort to reinvent himself after Tony Soprano in earnest.

His instinct was to do something real, and something local. And real life in his neighborhood had been changed forever during the third season of *The Sopranos* when two fully-loaded jetliners smashed into the World Trade Center, not two miles from his and Marcy's apartment in the West Village.

Susan Aston remembers coming to James's apartment after the planes hit. Power was out in places downtown, but Jim had electricity, and she, her niece Britney Houlihan, Jim, and Marcy hunkered down in front of the television after the towers fell and the tip of lower Manhattan went black with smoke and dust. Michael was still a toddler. They were joined later that day by Marcy's masseuse, Bethany Parish, and her husband Anthony; they lived in Battery Park City, right next to the towers, and Battery Park was being forcibly evacuated.

Like a lot of New Yorkers, they weren't sure that the attacks had ended. They saw out their windows the bedraggled lines of people in scorched clothes and with soot-blackened faces as they walked north from Ground Zero, very quietly for the most part, trying to find a way home. The bridges and tunnels were closed and all the subway and commuter trains shut off; Susan's then-husband, Mario Mendoza, had been upstate, and he'd parked his car north of Spuyten Duyvil and walked across the Henry Hudson Bridge into the city. Mario hitched rides or walked all the way down the island to join them in the Village that afternoon. They thought about getting the raft James had brought into the city from the Shore that summer. They could cross the river to Jersey, make their way quickly enough to friends' houses. At least there they could be mobile.

"But if we got the raft," James said, "we'd have to bring guns, too." They might need some means of defense if there was another attack—but also, perhaps, to ward off stranded commuters anxious to get off the island themselves. Aston says that's when she really started to freak out about what was happening.

They decided against making a dash across the river. Aston's mom called from Texas and told her that the Pentagon had been hit and another airliner had been crashed by its passengers in Pennsylvania. And that was it. But no one who was in New York City that day will ever forget the way it felt.

After the cleanup got underway, James, Tony Sirico, Vincent Pastore, and Vincent Curatola went to Ground Zero to meet with firemen, police, construction workers, and other volunteers to boost morale. The actors were mobbed.

"We were supposed to meet the mayor [Rudy Giuliani], but he couldn't make it, he got delayed, you know what it was like back then," Tony Sirico remembers. "So we go in, they gave us all these masks to wear, to breathe. There was like hundreds of these guys out there, and it was unbelievable, just unbelievable, what those buildings had become . . . Just twisted, what all was in it, well, you've seen the pictures. Unbelievable. And the guys who were working there were so happy to see us, any break from searching through that mess of wreckage, thinking you'd find a body. Only, they found out, there weren't many bodies.

"And at one point I took off my mask to light a cigarette, and *marone*," Sirico continues. "I almost choked. These guys were breathing that stuff day after day. . . . It was amazing. And I think [our commitment to do something for people responding to the attacks] all started from that. You just had to do something. We all felt it."

It's true, they did. The day after 9/11, Steve Buscemi, who the previous spring had directed Sirico in the acclaimed "The Pine Barrens" episode, in which Paulie Walnuts and Christopher Moltisanti get lost in the snow, had gone down to his old firehouse and volunteered. He spent a week clearing the rubble alongside his fellow firefighters.

Everything about those days became emotionally freighted for New Yorkers. At *The Sopranos*, they were careful to remove the brief glimpse of the towers you could catch in Tony's side rearview mirror as he left the Lincoln Tunnel during the credits sequence. Time was divided between the days when the World Trade Center was there and the days when it wasn't.

James told Susan that he felt ridiculous going to Ground Zero and just standing there in a mask, without really pitching in and helping, physically. But the overwhelming response of the working guys at Ground Zero, the way they so evidently loved the visit by Tony, Paulie, Big

Pussy, and Johnny Sack, revealed another side of this celebrity thing. It didn't have to be a fire hose aimed at you. It could be a spotlight you used to shine on other people.

Soon Gandolfini was going back to Jersey every fall for the annual OctoberWoman's Breast Cancer Foundation fund-raising dinner, to help out his old classmate Donna Mancinelli in Park Ridge. The whole cast came out to Bergen County, signing autographs and posing for pictures. Jim spent the night afterward, no matter how long the banquet took, drinking beer and telling jokes with his high school buddies in basements and rec rooms in Park Ridge.

Jim insisted on only HBO cameras, no media. But when the financial crash came in 2008, the cancer fund-raising changed—no one was buying thousand-dollar dinner tickets anymore—and *The Sopranos* had ended. What hadn't ended were the two wars sparked by the attack on the World Trade Center.

Those wars were still sending a steady stream of severely maimed and wounded soldiers back home. In 2006, Al Giordano, a former Marine and a veterans affairs activist, had helped found a nonprofit called the Wounded Warriors Project, designed to help returning soldiers adjust to civilian life. Part of the project was an annual summer event at Breezy Point, in Queens, where convalescent soldiers, including amputees, could get out in the sun, learn to use their prostheses, and do water sports—"like, learn to ski on one leg," Sirico, a vet himself, says. He called to find out if there was anything he could do, and Giordano invited him down.

"I had to do it, I just had to," Sirico says. "I mean, I play a tough guy, but these guys are the tough guys. After what they had done, I had to." He told Gandolfini about the event. Soon James was in touch with Giordano. Every July the Wounded Warriors mount a parade from Staten Island across the Verrazano Narrows Bridge and down to Breezy Point (the cops shut down the bridge and river traffic for the day). It's a long march of wounded soldiers, some more ambulatory than others. Gandolfini became a regular.

"Jim shows up in a red Cadillac convertible with a quadruple amputee, Eighty-second Airborne, his wife, daughter, and his mother-in-law in the backseat with him," Giordano recalls. This was in 2012. "And he drives them the whole parade route, it takes like two hours, and then spends the day at the beach. . . . I meet a lot of celebrities in my job, and some want to do this just for the cameras. But that was not Jim Gandolfini."

Gandolfini and Sirico toured military hospitals together, often with other actors from the show. They'd meet at Walter Reed hospital outside Washington, D.C., the Brooklyn Army Medical Center, and in rehab clinics around the Northeast, talking to large groups. Sirico remembers one Veterans Administration facility that had a rock-climbing wall, to help amputees regain a sense of mobility—many of them could climb to the top with just three, even two limbs. Gandolfini insisted on hooking up a belay harness and trying to climb in front of dozens of recovering soldiers.

"HBO woulda had a heart attack if they'd seen this," Sirico recalls. "So Jimmy gets all hooked up, he's like a really big guy then, and he climbs two, three, four handholds—and boom, flat on his ass! It brought down the house, I'm telling you."

They journeyed out to the U.S. military's chief burn center in San Antonio, always the most difficult place for a morale visit—soldiers with "half their face burned off, limbs burned off, in constant pain," Sirico recalls. "The trick is, never lose eye contact. I'd grab their arm, you know, where they weren't burned, touch them, let them know we care." Jim was representing an expensive watch company, and he would pass out $5,000 watches to the wounded—he'd hint that they didn't have to treat them like sentimental keepsakes if they needed the money.

All the soldiers knew who Tony Soprano was. DVDs of *The Sopranos* were popular items in Iraq and Afghanistan.

In 2006, HBO aired *Baghdad ER*, a documentary about life in a U.S. military trauma ward in Iraq, directed by Jon Alpert. The documentary was intense, heartbreaking, and profoundly honest, and it won a Peabody Award. Alpert wanted to do the obvious sequel, a documentary about soldiers returning and the work being done by Wounded Warriors. But HBO, perhaps understandably, thought however honorable the idea was, it was unlikely to draw an audience—eat-your-spinach TV is a euphemism here. Besides, the Pentagon had not liked *Baghdad ER*, and they decided to revoke the filmmaker's access to Walter Reed hospital just as he was about to shoot there.

That was when Gandolfini got involved. Although he didn't want to be on camera, an odd compromise evolved. The vets would come into New York City, to an empty stage set, and sit on a chair; Jim would sit off the dais, with the camera shooting over his shoulder, and interview them about their "Alive Day," the day they were wounded but survived.

Alive Day Memories: Home from Iraq became the first project Gandolfini put before the public after *The Sopranos* ended. He interviewed ten wounded soldiers, many of them missing two or three limbs, some with severe head trauma or post-traumatic stress syndrome. You don't hear much from Jim; occasionally you see him get up and hug the soldier when the interview is done. One of the subjects, former army first lieutenant Dawn Halfaker, a pretty redhead, had lost her right arm and shoulder to a rocket-propelled grenade. During their talk Halfaker wonders aloud whether her child, if she ever has one, could truly love her now. There's a long pause.

Gandolfini waits, waits a little longer, then quietly asks, "What were you just thinking about?"

"The reality of, will I be able to raise a kid?" she answers. "I won't be able to pick up my son or daughter with two arms."

Jim was committing a kind of journalism, though probably not the sort he'd imagined when he was getting that Rutgers degree. And it was also a kind of reversal on the celebrity journalism Gandolfini hated—he, the celebrity, out of the lights, real tough guys onstage and bearing witness to the awfulness of violence. Gandolfini kept in touch with some of the soldiers over time. He asked Giordano to help him find ways to help out. He wanted a Wounded Warrior driver for when he was in Los Angeles, and Giordano found him a marine vet who had once driven for a general.

Wounded Warriors became part of his crew. He filmed a series of public service announcements for the project just before he died, to help with fund-raising. (Wounded Warriors has now grown from Giordano and his two buddies into an organization with 421 direct employees and an annual budget of $200 million.) Giordano says he's not sure what to do with the PSAs now that Jim has died. But he remembers, when they were shooting the commercials and asked if he could do another take, Gandolfini replied, "Sure, this is way more important than the shit I usually do."

One of the wounded soldiers in *Alive Day* committed suicide a few years later. Jim had kept in touch. The vet set up his computer to send out farewell notes after he'd died, and Jim was one of the recipients.

Gandolfini teamed up with Alpert for a second documentary, this time as executive producer and narrator, on the history of wartime post-traumatic stress, *Wartorn 1861–2010*, in 2011. Tom Richardson of Attaboy Films says they were preparing a documentary on American prisons when Gandolfini died, and talking about a documentary on for-profit prisons. Alpert, like Sirico, became a regular visitor at the Jersey Shore in the summer, and Gandolfini took a seat on the board of his New York City documentary company.

In all his work on the documentaries and for charity, Jim was pretty consistent about trying to fade into the background.

"I grew up not so different than Jim," Al Giordano says. "I'm from Long Island. My dad was in the marines, I was in the marines, my brother went to West Point. Military service is in my family. I worked with Jim all these years, he was like a regular guy, you could talk with him about anything, he loved his Jets, Rutgers football, his son, his family, all of that, just like anybody. But I didn't know until I read about it, after he'd died, that his father had gotten a Purple Heart in World War II. He never mentioned it. And that kind of makes it all come together for me. He was quiet about certain things."

It's a reminder of what T. J. Foderaro called his "bullshit meter"—the way Jim would be embarrassed by any mention of his own problems, or any note of sympathy you might offer him (even about Lynn Jacobson's death). Gandolfini, Sirico, and Richardson—who'd met Buck twenty-five years earlier at the Rutgers pub—visited Iraq and Afghanistan together on U.S.O. tours. At first the U.S.O. put them up in a five-star hotel in Kuwait City, but Gandolfini wanted to see the war. They took off, first for a police station in Mosul, in Kurdistan, which had been taken back by American troops just the day before. They saw enough to make guys who play tough guys on TV respect the tough guys who were protecting them in the desert.

But they impressed everybody, even General Ray Odierno, a Jersey guy himself, who would later become commander of U.S. forces in Iraq. Giordano and the Wounded Warriors Project have decided to create an annual James Gandolfini Award, dedicated to the celebrity who does the most to support them in any year.

Gandolfini made two movies, too, in 2008, first David Chase's semiautobiographical *Not Fade Away,* about a young Italian-American growing up in Newark in the 1960s in love with the Rolling Stones. Gandolfini plays the slightly mystified father, whose son throws caution to the winds and heads to California with his upscale Jersey girlfriend—who promptly leaves him behind at a Malibu party to run off with Mick Jagger.

And Gandolfini played a world-weary American general in the British satire of the political shenanigans leading up to the Iraq war, *In the Loop.* The movie did rather well, appearing just as the American presidential elections were gearing up and the consensus that the war had been a huge mistake had hardened into a wide conviction. Gandolfini's is a supporting role, but one crucial to the plot, a U.S. general who knows the war will be a disaster but cynically comes out in support to help his career when he realizes Washington has already decided to go to war.

While he was filming *In the Loop*, Gandolfini caught some theater in the West End of London, including *The God of Carnage*, by French playwright Yasmina Reza. *Carnage* had debuted in Zurich, and it was being done in English by film star Ralph Fiennes, which was why Gandolfini chose to see it in the first place (well, that, and the fact that the play is only an hour and a half long). Gandolfini came out of the theater laughing and inspired. He met with the producers and broached the subject of bringing the play to Broadway.

He hadn't been on the New York stage since *A Streetcar Named Desire* with Alec Baldwin in 1992; he hadn't actually been *on stage* since 1997, when he did a short play at a ninety-nine-seat theater in Los Angeles run by Sean Penn's parents. But *The God of Carnage* was in many ways perfect: An ensemble piece with four equal parts, it tells the story of two fairly well-off couples who come together after their eleven-year-old sons have a fight at school. Gandolfini wanted to play the least neurotic character in the piece, a small-business owner married to an artsy wife (played by Marcia Gay Harden). Jeff Daniels played the

Fiennes part, an arrogant lawyer, whose wife (Hope Davis) "manages" her husband's wealth. The play is a high-voltage, quick-riposte comedy laced with raucous social satire (Daniels's character repeatedly talks on his cell phone with more attention than he does in person). Harden won the Tony, but it was Gandolfini who got the audience to show up. And he was very funny.

What happens in *The God of Carnage*—four adults coming together to discuss a fight between eleven-year-olds, who then wind up acting like middle-schoolers themselves—brought out his appealing childishness. Gandolfini was able to explode with deep frustration (something he did again and again on *The Sopranos*) to get laughs. And the play bristled with character reversals, the most important being the audience's sense that the lawyer's marriage was shaky is transferred to the small businessman's marriage over the course of the play.

But more to the point, *The God of Carnage* helped change Gandolfini's image in the business. "Comic roles started coming to him after *Carnage*," Mark Armstrong says. "He was offered the lead on *The Office* for its third incarnation, the part that ultimately James Spader took. He was very tempted, but it probably wouldn't have worked out, he had an exclusive contract with HBO. But we were getting more offers for comedy, and we were very happy with that."

In October 2009, Gandolfini married Deborah Lin in her native Honolulu, with hundreds of guests attending. The groom was forty-seven years old, the bride forty. They had just bought a colonial on almost nine acres for $1.5 million in the rolling hills around Tewksbury, New Jersey, about an hour from New York City. The house was new, built in 2007, and it won the New Jersey Builders Association Custom House of the Year Award, in part for its geothermal heating and cooling and the recycled, antique hardwood floors. Gandolfini commuted from Tewksbury to the city most days during *The God of Carnage*.

After taking a supporting role the next year as a New York City mayor in *The Taking of Pelham 1 2 3* (Gandolfini and Sirico had finally met Rudy Giuliani after the mix-up just after 9/11, and Sirico says they became good friends), Gandolfini returned to another childlike role. He played the voice for Carol, the big striped Wild Thing in *Where the Wild Things Are*, directed by Spike Jonze and adapted from the children's book by Maurice Sendak.

If *The God of Carnage* treated adults like children, *Where the Wild Things Are* treated children's fantasies like adult neuroses, and the little boy's relationship with Carol is key. Carol is sort of the child's id. We meet Carol (the character was played by another actor in a giant suit, and Jim synced his lines) as he's destroying the Wild Things' hivelike houses made of sticks; Carol shows Max his artwork, a stick-built version of the island where everyone can be happy. When Max finally leaves the island to go home, a tearful Carol begs him to stay, but knows he must go. All of this is only hinted at in Sendak's book, and the film adds a suggestive prestory about Max and his single mom, Connie (played by Catherine Keener), who is trying to date again (Mark Ruffalo). Gandolfini's sorrow over childhood's disappointments and ultimate loss is oddly powerful in the maw of the giant suit, and the message is more Eugène Ionesco than Lewis Carroll.

Gandolfini's friends say he was beginning to accept his status in Los Angeles now, too—the reflexive doubts about his ability to perform particular roles, and the letters to directors recommending other actors, had begun to fade from his practice. In 2010 he rented a house in Laurel Canyon, a twisting arroyo that is lined with expensive homes tucked into the sere California landscape. It's a relaxed enclave for movie business people, a beautiful section of green-friendly but often unpretentious houses that bring nature into their designs.

For the first time, Gandolfini begins to really go native in California. "Moving out here after those years in New York," says his manager Nancy Sanders, "he had a hard time with California for a while. Even at his Laurel Canyon home he'd see his neighbor just staring at the mountains for hours, and Jim would say, 'What the fuck is he looking at?'

"But he started to relax, I think," Sanders continues. "He was settling into the California lifestyle and caught himself enjoying some of it . . . except the driving. The thing about Jim was his mind never stopped. He'd think about things, sometimes too much. He was very bright, and with that comes a bit of being tortured and hard on yourself and others. I think in those last years he started to settle down and accept things a little better, realizing that he couldn't control it all."

"The doubts calmed down," says Mark Armstrong, Sanders's partner. "Jim was a pretty driven guy in some ways. He could yell at you when something went wrong, but he'd hug you when it was over, that was his way of communicating, you know? But he seemed much more accepting in those last couple of years."

And in 2010 Gandolfini released a film that reads like an act of love, *Welcome to the Rileys*, about a small businessman from Indianapolis and his wife of thirty years (Melissa Leo) whose daughter died in a car accident years before. The couple has drifted apart as the wife's guilt turns into an intense agoraphobia, and Doug Riley wanders into an affair with a waitress. On a convention trip to New Orleans for his plumbing supply business, Riley meets a sixteen-year-old stripper and runaway (Kristen Stewart of *Twilight* fame) and decides to sell his business and live with her, platonically, almost like a replacement dad. When his wife overcomes her lassitude and joins him in New Orleans, she, too, accepts the stripper, and they form an uneasy pseudo-family until the girl bolts. But the effort reunites the older couple, and allows them to accept life once more.

Directed by Jake Scott, the son of Ridley and nephew of Tony, *Welcome to the Rileys* debuted at the 2010 Sundance Festival, where some critics cited it as part of Gandolfini's continuing effort to "whack Tony Soprano." It is that, of course, but it's also an extension of his everyman persona, another small businessman (like his part in *The God of Carnage*) and a confused soul lost in the middle of his life. Tony without the gang and violence, you have to say.

Gandolfini had contemplated the problem of how to make his break from the gangster genre during *The God of Carnage*, telling *The Los Angeles Times* that the audience might not have accepted him "in a wig as Ferdinand II" right after *The Sopranos* ended ("I'd pay to see that," costar Jeff Daniels quipped). Generals and big-city mayors were not that far from Tony, in some ways; small businessmen from Brooklyn and then Indianapolis were yet another step away.

There was still a problem of scale, somehow, with Gandolfini's presence in a film. A lot of TV stars have difficulty transferring to the movies—it's like the audience doesn't want to let you disappear into a different character. They think they know you, and they want to see you, not someone else. Gandolfini could overcome this problem to an extent; he could bring an audience to a sophisticated comedy, as *The God of Carnage* showed. But as part of a coequal quartet, he was like a bass player doing lead guitar. The contemporary movie with a character actor as its lead was a rare thing, and finding just the right part was harder than it looked.

After studying the problems of runaway kids for *Welcome to the Rileys*, in 2011, Gandolfini heard a radio report about a home for runaways and abused kids in Toms River, near the Jersey Shore, called Ocean's Harbor House. It's a twelve-bed shelter that's open twenty-four-hours a day every day, with medical services and counseling as well as food and clothing for ten- to nineteen-year-olds.

Michael's school in L.A. had asked its students to do some form of community service in the summer and report on it in the fall. So Gandolfini called Harbor House to see if he and Michael could help out in any way. The director said they had no computers for the kids—would Gandolfini care to contribute toward that?

Jim took Michael, who was eleven at the time, to a nearby electronics outlet and bought thirteen laptops, which he and Michael loaded with software and drove over to drop off. While Michael showed the computers to the kids and counselors, Jim walked the grounds. The garden and property were scraggly with weeds after the Jersey summer.

The next day Jim hired workmen at a nearby lawn center to pull the weeds and vines, and then he and Michael trucked over with eight yards of mulch. The image of Jamie helping his father at the Catholic high school in Paramus with maintenance and painting chores comes immediately to mind. They spent the afternoon spreading the mulch with the help of facilities director Ken Butterworth.

Gandolfini was, Butterworth remembers, "completely down-to-earth, really likable. Approachable, you know? You could tell he really loved his kid, and wanted him to know that not everybody is lucky with their families.

"And so we were working together, and I asked him, 'Where'd you go to college?'" Butterworth says. "And he looked away, I think he said Rutgers, but I thought, 'Ah, so we're not going to talk about you, huh?'"

Knowing where the boundaries should be was becoming more important every year. Gandolfini had been working with his acting coach, Harold Guskin, on an independent film, called *Kiddie Ride*, written by Guskin's wife, Sandra Jennings, that was all about boundaries. Set at the Jersey Shore and debuting at a 2011 film festival, it got limited release as *Down the Shore* in 2013 (though that was not Guskin's edit). Jennings wrote the script with Gandolfini in mind. There were autobiographical elements—the Shore of course, the working middle-class milieu and so on. The conflict stems from the hero's sense of loyalty and friendship, which keep him from claiming what's rightfully his.

Bailey (Gandolfini) runs the merry-go-round and kiddie train concession in a cheap seaside carnival. His best friend owns it all, including the girl next door, Mary (Famke Janssen), who was Bailey's first love.

Most of the movie takes place in the little step-back houses built chock-a-block in Keansburg, not so different from those in nearby Lavallette, where Jim's parents summered when he was a kid. (Half of Keansburg's 3,300 houses were destroyed or damaged by Hurricane Sandy in 2012, lending the film an archival sadness.) Bailey and Mary used to crawl across the tiny gap between their houses on a ladder laid across their bedroom windowsills.

The plot turns on family secrets, a murder, financial schemes, and drugs, all familiar Jersey themes from *The Sopranos*, but here the crime occurred years before our story begins. At the conclusion Bailey, Mary, and her mentally handicapped son are in a truck with a bag full of money and the highway in front of them, about as Elmore Leonard-y an ending as you could want (Gandolfini loved crime novels and thrillers, Leonard's and Stephen Hunter's most of all). Unlike *The Sopranos*, there is hope, but only in escape from New Jersey—Bailey and Mary have a second chance at happiness if they drive all night.

Guskin and Jennings have nothing but praise for Gandolfini's acting as Bailey, but the most significant aspect for a student of his career is that it's his first romantic lead. Maybe that's why *Variety* called it "James Gandolfini's most substantial feature role to date." It works in part because we're left to imagine the two lovers as teenagers and all the years before the story begins. Whether it's his "enduring status as a sex symbol" or just a function of his gift, the contrast between Janssen and Gandolfini— the svelte former model, famous at the time for her performance as Jean Grey, heartthrob of the *X-Men* series, and a now "270-pound Woody Allen" as Jim described himself the year before—never registers as an impediment to their romance. We take it for granted that she loves him.

Like a lot of indie films, there was trouble with the financing in the wake of the 2008 financial collapse, so *Kiddie Ride/Down the Shore*, like *Romance & Cigarettes*, never got quite the attention it deserved. But the project was important to Gandolfini, and he felt bad enough about the outcome to ask Guskin and Jennings if they were "okay with money" after it went awry. "Can you imagine anyone else saying that?" Jennings says. "We'll be fine, but that's not the point. That was Jim. He could have made oodles of money instead of taking his time to do this film, and then he asks us if *we're* all right."

"Acting was his family," Guskin says, beaming.

Family and acting had to be what Gandolfini was thinking about. His other project in 2011 was *Cinema Verite*, a TV film for HBO about the making of *An American Family*, the PBS documentary series about Bill and Pat Loud, a well-to-do couple in Santa Barbara, California, and their five handsome kids. *An American Family*, which aired in 1973, is usually thought to be the ultimate ancestor of reality TV. Gandolfini plays documentarian Craig Gilbert, who discovered the Louds and convinced them to try the "bold experiment" of putting their lives on TV. What he ends up making, of course, is an exposé of the family's dissolution, brought on in part by the pressures of having a film crew document their daily lives.

Gandolfini plays Gilbert with a wonderful ambiguity. Gilbert himself never made another film after *An American Family*: The series was a huge ratings success, but it also led to a heavy round of media condemnation, for the Louds as a family but also for Gilbert, his methods, and the meaning of what he had achieved. Was an entertaining documentary on the breakup of a successful, liberal California family worth the breakup itself? Was the American fame culture corrosive of family values?

The fact that eldest son Lance Loud came out as gay on the show—essentially the first openly gay man on American TV—and ended up as an editor and writer for Andy Warhol's *Interview* magazine only underlined the profundity of these themes. Lance died of AIDS in 2001, and, as *Cinema Verite* reveals in its credits, his last wish was for his parents to get back together. And they did.

There were all sorts of fascinating aspects to the story of the making of *An American Family*, but what everyone in the media has always agreed about was Craig Gilbert's role: he was the serpent in the garden.

Gandolfini said he saw the man differently. "I've gone to lunch with [Gilbert] a few times in New York City," Jim, ever diligent about his research, told the press at the premiere. "He's a wonderful man, smart, honest, incredibly intelligent. Old-fashioned way about him, graduated from Harvard. He was an ambulance driver in World War II— he's old school. I enjoy him immensely. I love the guy.

"This experience really hurt him," Gandolfini continued. "I think he was so astounded that the Loud family got so destroyed and he got so destroyed by people. They went after the Loud family so viciously. All they were really were regular people and their family was not that much different than anybody else's. He was just trying to document it and they went after both of them so viciously that he said, 'The hell with this.'"

As it happened, *Cinema Verite* hurt, too. As written, the script broadly hinted that Gilbert and Pat Loud had an affair during the filming of *An American Family*. Before shooting began Gilbert hired a lawyer to watch over his and the Louds' interests, but there is nonetheless a scene in which Diane Lane, as Pat Loud, follows Gandolfini, as Gilbert, to his hotel room to see evidence of her husband's infidelity. And in a gesture familiar from scores of movies beginning with D. W. Griffith, Gandolfini reaches out and places his hand on Lane's. Fade to black.

HBO paid the Louds a settlement with the stipulation that they never discuss the film, but Gilbert refused. It didn't help that suspicion about his relationship with Pat Loud had been part of the original controversy in 1973. Gilbert was bitter about how it turned out, and complained to *The New Yorker* about *Cinema Verite* in April 2011. Now eighty-five and living in the same one-room apartment on Jane Street in Manhattan that he'd had for twenty-one years, Gilbert said he'd told Gandolfini at dinner "no in twenty ways" about the old rumor of an affair. Pat Loud has also consistently denied the rumors.

Truth, art, privacy, telling a good story—they can get tangled up so easily. You can use the word "damn," but there's no question that *An American Family* did something with four letters to the Louds. So it's a metaphor, allowed under an artist's license.

In *Cinema Verite* there's a scene in which Gandolfini-Gilbert meets with a tableful of suits from PBS about his cost overruns and dull drama—would the show end up ten hours of "pass the salt?" Gandolfini wears a flippy seventies-era toupee, and struggles not to sound unctuous as he asks for patience. You have to build trust with a family before the drama begins, he says. Gandolfini, as a character actor, was stretching himself to portray the man whose work, inadvertently or not, had helped create "reality TV" and all its attendant assaults on norms of privacy. He was, in a way, siding with the "vampires" in the press—and at the same time invading the privacy of a creative filmmaker, albeit one who could never work again.

"[Gilbert] tried to do something that nobody else had ever done," Gandolfini said. "It ended up this exceptional thing. Then they threw out all the rest of the footage, hours and hours, they threw it all out—and he was incredibly hurt by all of it.

"He's a bit of a freak—but a great guy. He tells me what an asshole I am every time he sees me. 'You're an asshole Jim, you're an idiot.' I say, 'You're absolutely right,' and I laugh—he's a charming man."

The reminder of the sharp edge of fame *Cinema Verite* delivered was ironic, perhaps, but it may have left a bruise.

The next year Gandolfini took a small part, as C.I.A. chief Leon Panetta, in the celebrated movie about SEAL Team Six and the killing of Osama bin Laden, *Zero Dark Thirty*. Gandolfini did his research, and achieved a plausible resemblance to the former California congressman. The movie was controversial, however, for the suggestion that torture had led to cracking the bin Laden case (it's a long and complicated argument that in no way hurt the box office). But Jim took no chances.

When Panetta retired from his subsequent post as President Barack Obama's secretary of defense, he told ABC News's Martha Raddatz that Gandolfini actually wrote him a note apologizing for his portrayal. Panetta recalled the note saying, "As an Italian I'm sure, you know, you probably have a lot of concerns about how I played your role." Panetta had questioned the accuracy of the overall film, but as far as Jim was concerned, he was simply glad that "thank God it was an Italian."

"The reality is, I like him, I like him as an actor," Panetta told Raddatz. "I've met him before, and he did a great job in the movie."

Remember, even as *The Sopranos* fell four or five years into the past, every time a former cast member picked his nose (or, okay, stood by while a New York City police officer was shot, or hired a Gambino family goon to collect a debt) there would be a headline about life imitating art again. Having played Tony Soprano so well for so long was like sowing a minefield through your future. You could not do anything in public that might in even the wildest imagination seem vaguely Tony-like without getting accused of imitating art. Or worse, justifying the way people sometimes looked frightened at your approach.

Guskin says that Gandolfini came to him in 2012 about a part in a movie that Brad Pitt had asked Jim to do, *Killing Them Softly,* that he'd agreed to as a favor but wasn't sure he really wanted to go through with. The movie is based on a novel by George Higgins, a bleak chronicler of the Irish mob in Boston best known for *The Friends of Eddie Coyle,* a 1973 movie with Robert Mitchum. Higgins's vision of a criminal is much more Whitey Bulger than Bobby Baccala.

Killing Them Softly is set in New Orleans, where Pitt lives. He plays a hard-bitten hitman for the mob who prefers to kill his victims "softly," by shooting them when they won't see it coming and will feel no pain or panic. But he happens to know his next victim personally, so he hires Mickey Fallon, played by Gandolfini, to do it for him.

Guskin says Gandolfini thought he was "done" with such violent characters forever, but as he thought about the alcoholic, dissolute nature of the part, he began to see how the role might whack the very idea of his playing a mobster ever again. Mickey Fallon (Fini's Irishness is entirely notional here) takes shape in two long, rambling conversations with Pitt, in a bar and in Mickey's hotel suite, where they discuss means and methods of the trade. Fallon's lechery and drunkenness is so grotesque that Pitt's character tips off the police, who nab Mickey on an old weapons charge before he can attempt a kill.

Like everything based on Higgins's writing, the movie is sourly depressing—not inappropriate for a picture about murder for hire, surely. And Gandolfini works hard to expunge the least wisp of charm from his presence: pale, puffy-faced, and breathing stertorously, he's a study in depravity. It was, indeed, the last hitman he would ever play.

On October 10, 2012, James and Deb had a baby daughter in Los Angeles. They christened her Liliana Ruth. Jim told Armstrong and Sanders he liked working on movies that his kids would want to see—that was the original idea he had for *Where the Wild Things Are*.

He'd been working at the end of that year on a big Hollywood comedy, *The Incredible Burt Wonderstone*, with Steve Carell, Steve Buscemi, and Jim Carrey. It was about the way magic acts were becoming weird endurance feats, a kind of performance art for hip audiences, leaving established Las Vegas magicians looking lame. Gandolfini plays an increasingly frustrated agent for Carell and Buscemi.

"It was a chance to work with two of the biggest comedians in Hollywood," Armstrong says, "and it was a character." *Wonderstone* got disappointing reviews, and had the worst opening box office of any Carell or Carrey movie yet. Gandolfini was filming, but in March 2013 Armstrong went with Michael to the red carpet premiere of *The Incredible Burt Wonderstone* in Los Angeles. They were already planning their trip to Rome that June.

10.

Beloved

How do you describe what *The Sopranos*, and in particular Tony Soprano, meant to New Jersey?

Of course there were the politicians who paid tribute when Gandolfini died, Governor Chris Christie of New Jersey first of all. He had all state flags flown at half-mast, called Gandolfini "a true Jersey guy" in the official statement, and showed his respect at the funeral at Saint John the Divine in Manhattan. Christie is forever auditioning for the role of "regular Jersey guy" himself, and there are those who question whether a politician with, shall we say, so well-rounded a personality could have been elected in the twenty-first century without the example of a certain 270-pound Woody Allen. Newark mayor and now senator Cory Booker tweeted that Jim was "a true NJ Great and NJ Original." Secretary of State John Kerry helped expedite the body's return from Rome; many others expressed their sorrow and shock in different ways.

Bruce Springsteen was playing a concert in London

when he heard the news, and he dedicated a straight play-through of his breakthrough album, *Born to Run,* to Gandolfini from the stage, the New Jersey equivalent of a twenty-one-gun salute.

Great honors, all of them, but not exactly the final word. Holsten's ice cream parlor in Bloomfield made a shrine of the table where Tony and his family faded to black, putting a RESERVED sign on the Formica with a vase of flowers and a copy of the Thursday afternoon *Star-Ledger* carrying front-page notice of Gandolfini's death in Rome.

The Star-Ledger, the newspaper where I worked for fifteen years, covered both the private funeral service in Park Ridge and the public one at Saint John's like they were writing about JFK's coffin on Lincoln's original catafalque. It's not surprising really. The newspaper itself was a character on *The Sopranos.* Tony ambled down his driveway in that bathrobe to pick it up at the start of many episodes. One of the show's neatest reversals was having Carmela run down the drive to get the Sunday *Ledger* first, so she could sift through all the sections and pluck out the lifestyles feature showing Uncle Junior was living in a state home for non compos mentis patients. She didn't want to upset Tony, who at that point wanted to have his uncle killed.

The mutual admiration between the newspaper and *The Sopranos* was part of the satire, part of the show's wink at reality. But it was also a natural fit, both institutions seeing themselves as being in the business of bringing unpleasant truths to a broad middle-class audience (one perhaps more entertainingly than the other). David Chase had gotten his start in Hollywood with a TV series called *Kolchak: The Night Stalker*, about a Chicago newspaperman who keeps uncovering unbelievable supernatural events. For *The Sopranos*, *The Star-Ledger* was credited for technical advice; many of the plotlines seemed to come straight from newspaper stories, like Big Pussy's idea to create fake HMO clinics to defraud Medicaid, or padding downtown esplanade contracts with no-show jobs for wiseguys.

There was, as well, the odd coincidence of all those old friends of Gandolfini's who worked at the paper, like account executive Vito Bellino, who held that horse's costume in the Rutgers football ads, and T. J. Foderaro, who was wine critic at the paper for a time. Not to mention Mark Di Ionno, in his columns often the voice of exactly those same regular Jersey guys that Gandolfini said he wanted to stand up for.

"He never left New Jersey," Di Ionno says of Gandolfini. "That's how he came and went. I think that's an interesting aspect of his power. . . . I don't think that James Gandolfini would have ever chosen to reinvent himself. There's too much in his wake, there's too many people who know the real man."

He was grounded, in other words, by his native state. When he was asked once whether it made any difference to him, shooting in places where he grew up and had so much personal history, Gandolfini said, "it maybe makes it a bit less glamorous." Not being glamorous is a good working definition of "grounded."

"But the most interesting thing about *The Sopranos* in this state was the way they accepted it," Di Ionno continues. "It's like the way my father and my uncle went to see *The Godfather*. They saw it as [about] Italians first, and gangsters second. . . . There were protests, sure, and some towns wouldn't let *The Sopranos* shoot within their districts. But in the end, it didn't matter."

Giovanna Pugliesi is a librarian at *The Star-Ledger*, and her family had a direct experience with the show in a way you always hear about along Guinea Gulch. One day around Christmas, a site finder stopped in to ask Giovanna's parents if they'd let *The Sopranos* film a scene in their house. I ask Giovanna why they chose her parents' house, and she says, "Because it looks so Italian."

It's a house on a corner lot in Clifton, right on the border of Montclair, one of the more upscale suburbs on Bloomfield Avenue. Montclair is where Stephen Colbert and, it sometimes seems, half the editorial staff at *The New York Times* live. So why did it look so "Italian"?

"Well," Giovanna says, "there's a fountain in the front yard. . . ."

Not to mention a big wooden spoon on the wall in the hallway to the kitchen—Giovanna says the big wooden spoon that no one ever uses was a marker of Italianness on *Everybody Loves Raymond*. The crew for *The Sopranos* came and spent two and a half days—they'd originally said it would take two—and Mr. and Mrs. Pugliesi loved it.

First the crew brought handheld heaters to melt all the snow in the front yard (the episode was supposed to be set in the early fall). Then they sanitized the interior of any family possessions that might get them sued later, like photos or awards. They even removed a painting on a wall, in case the artist might object. All these preparations were necessary, and performed at every location the show set up; the location shots are what made *The Sopranos* one of the most expensive TV productions of its time, even though its "exotic locale" was just across the river on suburban avenues and cul-de-sacs.

Then they shot their scene. Stevie Van Zandt, as Tony's consigliere Silvio Dante, knocks on the door, and Artie Pasquale, playing Burt Gervasi, a Lupertazzi family soldier, lets him in. They talk, and Silvio sneaks up behind Burt and garrotes him in the Pugliesis' living room. It's a very violent scene, as graphic as anything in *The Sopranos.* The episode was the second to last of the series, called "The Blue Comet," because it concludes with Bobby Baccalieri (Steve Schirripa) getting shot to death in a model train store (the Blue Comet was a famous passenger train that used to run between Philadelphia and Atlantic City).

Giovanna says her mom didn't really mind that it was such a violent scene—"Is no real," Giovanna laughed, imitating her mom's voice.

"It was exciting," she says. "They were shooting this TV show that everybody all across the country was watching, and it was set here, in New Jersey. It was about Italians. What's not to love?"

The Sopranos was a show about antiglamor, about this out-of-the-way state that never gets any respect, and it was making all the places it shot look glamorous (at least, in retrospect). James Gandolfini was just a regular New Jersey guy playing a not-so-regular Jersey guy, a murderer, in fact, but that was glamorous, too. James Bond is just a suit with a gun. *The Simpsons* once did an episode about that, how a gun in anybody's hand, even Marge's, makes them look stylish, cool, glamorous.

Throughout the run of *The Sopranos,* network executives worried that David Chase's bleak sense of humor would ruin the whole thing. Early in the first season they knew they had in Tony a character Americans found fascinating, even lovable. Then Chase had him murder that Mafia snitch he'd glimpsed while driving Meadow to visit potential colleges, or had him beat one of his big, genial, but terminally stupid wiseguys unconscious with a phone. How could a television audience continue to love Tony after he did something like that? Archie Bunker would not have survived turning Meathead in for smoking pot in the basement—would folks tune in after their hero had murdered somebody, or terrified them with his uncontrolled viciousness?

They stayed with Tony, of course, in spite of the violence.

And that's largely because of Gandolfini's remarkable ability to grab your sympathy. But it was also because the audience *The Sopranos* had found was not the same as the audience that watched *Bonanza* or *The Brady Bunch*. For that matter, the United States wasn't the same country that produced those shows. We weren't all riding some wagon train to the stars together anymore; there was a lot more sympathy for the devil then there used to be.

The key to Tony's appeal was explicitly defined in the third season, during an episode called "Employee of the Month," which dealt with the rape of Tony's psychiatrist, Dr. Jennifer Melfi, played by Lorraine Bracco. Her brutal rape was one of those signature *Sopranos* scenes of scarifying violence, the sort you almost never see on TV. Dr. Melfi files a complaint, and the rapist is arrested. But the cops have to let him go because of some technicality, and when Melfi sees him working in a fast-food restaurant, she's shocked to see his picture framed on the wall as "Employee of the Month."

Later she meets her own analyst, Dr. Elliot Kupferberg (played by director Peter Bogdanovich), and tells him about the anger and frustration, not to mention simmering fear, that the experience left her. And she goes on to describe a strange dream in which she walks out of her consulting office and tries to get a soda from a vending machine, but it doesn't come and she gets her arm trapped in the opening. There's a Rottweiler barking nearby. Suddenly she sees her rapist in the room, he begins to assault her again, and the dog leaps on him as he cries in fear and pain.

"Oh my god, the dog," she says to her analyst (the script is by Robin Green and Mitchell Burgess). "A Rottweiler, Elliot. Big head, massive shoulders, the direct descendant of the dogs bred by Roman soldiers to guard their camps."

Bogdanovich murmurs, "I didn't know that. . . ."

"Who could I sic on that son of a bitch to tear him to shreds?" she continues. "Let me tell you something, no feeling has ever been so sweet as to see that pig beg and plead and scream for his life. Because the justice system is fucked up, Elliot. . . . Who's going to fix it, you, Elliot?"

Of course, no shrink could fix anything in the way her psyche wants revenge—no modern, civilized male could do it for her, either. But Tony Soprano could. He would want to do it for her. All she needs to do is tell him.

It's an echo of the famous wedding scene in *The Godfather*, when Don Vito Corleone agrees to have the man who beat up the undertaker's daughter severely beaten himself, in return for a service the Godfather will ask for later. (That service turns out to be fixing up Sonny Corleone's machine-gunned corpse for burial.) Private justice has always been the mob's self-justification—they police the crimes the mainstream courts can never adequately address.

This is where gangster movies meet a deep American need to explain the country's failure to achieve perfect justice. If democracy and civic education are so wonderful, if the Founding Fathers wrote a Constitution that perfects the hodgepodge of inherited political traditions brought here from Europe, why is there crime at all? At least, why is there so *much* crime?

All American antiheroes claim vigilantism as an excuse sooner or later—they all want to be the Batman. The Mafia does, too. But they're not Bruce Wayne. Gangsters have achieved a certain social position at different times in history. When the British annexed Singapore, they decided to exclude the Chinese tongs from the mines, reasoning that they exploited the workers and made their lives miserable. But without the Chinese gangsters, the labor markets became unmanageable. There were strikes, violent struggles between factions, pitched battles in the mines themselves. Quietly, the British invited the Triads and their enforcers back. Gang kingpins took to nice estates in the hills, and had toddies with their British neighbors out of sight of either community.

The Mafia was never that important to American labor, but at the height of unionization after the war, they counted for something. Today, that whole world of unionized labor, big pension funds—pensions themselves—is gone, or disappearing. People loved Tony Soprano because he seemed to be able to do something about all that, maybe turn the clock back a little. Even if it was only to highjack a shipment of flat-screen TVs that would otherwise have gone into shopping centers for the rich. It was nice just to imagine a working-class guy with power.

Dr. Melfi's moment of Mafia sympathy passes. She

tells her analyst, "Don't worry, I'm not going to break the social compact," and she never tells Tony about her rapist.

But some of the affection for that "big head, massive shoulders" that she expressed in "Employee of the Month" underwent a kind of psychological transference to James Gandolfini. Because even if he had the bottomless hurt and hair-trigger temper of Stanley Kowalski, deep down you knew he was Mitch. Sweet, dependable, *respectable* Mitch.

New York had a white Christmas in 2010—a *really* white Christmas. After a dusting, a few inches, fell on Christmas Eve, the day after the holiday it started to snow. And snow. The city plows were overwhelmed; Bedford Street in Tribeca went unplowed over the weekend. Monday night around 8:00 P.M., a driver tried to use Bedford to make a shortcut onto Christopher Street that turned into spinning wheels in what amounted to a three-foot drift.

Luckily for the driver, right behind him in his four-wheel-drive SUV was Tony Soprano. James Gandolfini climbed out of his car and started rocking the stranded driver's car back and forth to give him traction. There was so much snow it didn't help much at first. People along Bedford started gathering to watch—it wasn't every day you saw a TV and Broadway star looking for cardboard scraps to put under a back tire. A handful of folks started to help. Almost by main force, forty-five minutes later they got the car out of the drift and moving unsteadily down the street. Cheers. Then Gandolfini ducked into the nearby Daddy-O tavern and broke a $100 bill to give $20 tips to all the guys who helped.

Cheers again.

It's not much, really. Any of us would do the same, especially if our car was behind the stranded driver. James would never have mentioned it.

But the *New York Post* did. And then, so did the TV stations and gossip channels. Sometimes fame is ugly, but sometimes it's just mindless chatter about everyday events that nonetheless undermine or confirm a larger sense about a celeb. Saving the driver in a Christmas week snowdrift became one of those stories.

No one knew, at this point, about James giving every regular actor on *The Sopranos* a $33,000 personal check in 2004. The OctoberWoman's Foundation fund-raising for breast cancer research was only dimly perceived, largely because James himself had forbidden journalists and TV outlets from covering it. His work with Wounded Warriors was public, of course, but not that well known in 2010. But the snowdrift on Bedford Street went around the world in an instant.

Actually, James's friends had noted this public citizen thing of his for a while, sometimes with mild annoyance. T. J. Foderaro recalls going out with his friend for long walks in Manhattan after closing time and dreading the possibility of coming across a wino lying on the sidewalk;

Jim might very easily decide that it was going to get cold, or rain that night, and they should stop and help the guy get home, or to a shelter. There went the night's conversation.

All those years as a bouncer may have had something to do with it. Club managers see all kinds of people in all kinds of states, and their job is to make sure every customer has a good time but can get out the door in one piece. The job itself is about taking responsibility.

Anyway, James was the kind of person you could count on in a pinch like that, and he took it with him to Hollywood, too. Tony Lipin is a film producer in Los Angeles now, but when he first met Gandolfini, on the set of *Crimson Tide* in 1994, he was working as a costumer. He dressed Jim as a Navy lieutenant. Lipin worked with Gandolfini a few times more as a costumer.

In 1997, William Friedkin signed on to do a remake of *Twelve Angry Men* for television featuring Jack Lemmon and George C. Scott, and Lipin was hired to do the costumes. That was a good year for Jim, before his breakthrough on *The Sopranos* but after he felt he had a solid career going as a character actor. He got the part of juror number six, the house painter who tries to get everyone to stay calm and get along.

"I had a chance to see he had a big heart at a cocktail party when we finished shooting *Twelve Angry Men*, a party held really to celebrate a great cast," Lipin says. In addition to Lemmon, Scott, and Gandolfini, Hume

Cronyn, Edward James Olmos, Ossie Davis, Tony Danza, and William Petersen are among the actors. "Bill [Friedkin] wanted us to mark it somehow, so the whole crew gathered for drinks."

Scott was great in his part, the small businessman who holds out for a guilty verdict because of his personal regret about the loss of his own son (Lee J. Cobb in the original). But these were the years, toward the end of his life, when Scott was pretty lost in his alcoholism.

"The party was winding down, really there were almost no people left, but Scott was totally out of it, lying on a couch," Lipin recalls. "And it came down to Jim, Petersen, and me to carry Scott out to the town car the production had provided for him. There was no way he could get home on his own. What struck me was the quiet way Jim helped Scott to his feet and got us to take him down and gently lay him in the backseat, no fuss, just simple acceptance. . . ."

One of Gandolfini's favorite writers was Charles Bukowski, the Los Angeles poet of the poor, drunks, and the drudgery of taking a straight job. But Jim's solicitousness for another actor in his cups wasn't literary. Clearly he understood drunkenness, not just from his time in the clubs but from personal experience (1997 was also the year Gandolfini got arrested for drag racing while drunk).

Part of Gandolfini's charisma flowed from a romantic fatalism, a kind of hoping against hopelessness. Several of Jim's Rutgers friends mentioned his affection for a fellow

student back then who everyone knew as "John the Arab."
John actually had an Italian surname, but his father worked
for an oil company in Saudi Arabia when John was growing up, and when the kid enrolled at Rutgers one of his
distinguishing accomplishments was the ability to imitate
the muezzin's chant from a minaret perfectly. At least, perfectly as far as the ears of a bunch of Jersey sophomores in
New Brunswick could discern. Hence, John the Arab.

Thing was, not very many of Jim's crew liked John that
much. He was rather withdrawn; he could be inexplicably
rude, and some of the coeds thought he was "creepy." But
Jim sympathized with John. He was always hanging at
the Birchwood apartment because Jim told him he was
welcome. When John finally had a kind of psychic break,
Jim took him over to mental health services. Almost nobody visited John in the convalescent ward, but Jim did,
often dragging a friend or two along with him. It was those
friends who told me the story of John the Arab, looking
back on it as one of the strangest things about their friend
Buck.

Tom Richardson says Gandolfini kept bringing John
up after breaking through in Hollywood. "Where's John
the Arab?" he'd ask, and when Richardson came to work
at Attaboy Films in 2009, he actually started a search. He
couldn't find him. An Italian-American who can imitate
the Muslim call to prayer—how hard could it be to find
someone like that? But they never did.

Still, that dogged loyalty to the old days is something

that evokes loyalty in return. One way friends showed loyalty was by never talking to the press; many of them kept the faith after Gandolfini's death by refusing to go on the record for this book. Yet even as they refused, they'd shake their heads and wonder out loud why—they really had only the nicest things to say. But really, there were no smoking guns or anything, they all say that with real conviction. The Gandolfinis, the whole family, they'd say, were just "very private."

"I can't say I know that for certain, but my impression of him was that as he became more famous he was really uncomfortable with all that attention," Di Ionno told me. "There was a part of him that I don't think really, really got it. I don't think it was a completely false humility. Maybe it was more scary than that. Maybe it was a sense of, like, 'I'm not really entitled to this . . . my mother was a cafeteria lady, my father was a school janitor, I know what I am deep down inside—I'm a regular guy who got really lucky.'"

Di Ionno was one of the early crew who'd lost touch, but he was easy enough to find when *The Sopranos* did its location shoot for the pilot episode. Jim invited Mark over to the set, and they had a hugging reunion. It was Hometown Boy Makes Good. Di Ionno says they picked up talking like no time had passed at all, though they hadn't seen each other for more than a decade.

Many of the others—Richardson, Bellino, Mark Ohlstein, Stewart Lowell, Tony Foster, and some of the Park

Ridge friends, like Ken Koehler, Donna Mancinelli, and her two brothers—had kept in touch. They'd come down to the Shore in the summer, had their kids play together. Susan Aston, of course, worked with Jim pretty directly for over twenty-five years, as did Harold Guskin. All of them acted protective of Jim's memory, as if he were incongruously defenseless or vulnerable. It's hard to believe that so many people would react so similarly, with such emotional directness, if they were trying to mislead.

Jim gave Di Ionno invitations to *The Sopranos* premiere, and the invites kept coming. *The Star-Ledger* itself sponsored a reception for the whole cast just as the first season ended on air. By then, everybody knew the show was going to be a phenomenon.

"At the second season premiere [in New York City]—and I'll never forget this—he was walking out, and there's people lined up behind the velvet rope yelling for him," Di Ionno remembers. "'Tony, hey, Tony! Hey, Tony!' And this cloud kind of passed over his face. He was smiling and stuff, but I just got this sense that he was thinking to himself, 'They don't know what the fuck I am, I'm a TV character.' And frankly even our newspaper treated him like they couldn't separate Tony Soprano from James Gandolfini."

It really was a kind of love. The kind an audience enjoys.

"How Italian was he?" one of Jim's oldest friends once replied, when I asked the obvious question. "Well, he was Italian enough to refuse spaghetti sauce from a can. Wouldn't touch the stuff. The sauce had to be real. But he was American enough to use ketchup at the table if it wasn't tomatoe-y enough."

Food authenticity has become a yardstick of Italian authenticity. Mario Batali, Jim's old friend from Rutgers, made a very successful career of it. Hand-dipped mozzarella, hand-tied bracciole, hand-cut pastas, and handpicked tomatoes are the secret. The old ways are the best.

As he grew successful, he became a regular at Batali's restaurants, and he always had an eye for fine food and wine. But he also had simple tastes. Friends told me James liked macaroni and cheese, for example. As someone who lived in the same pre-Giuliani Manhattan in the 1980s, they sound like bachelor tastes to me. He liked to eat, that was clear, but was more a gourmand than a gourmet, with that tinge of overeating the first word implies.

His friends listed a dozen movies as his favorites, more than half of them comedies (*Borat*, *The Odd Couple*, *The Great Outdoors*, *Role Models*, *It's a Mad, Mad, Mad, Mad World*, the original version of *The Producers*). He also loved Dom DeLuise's *Fatso*, about an Italian boy who grows up fat because every time he gets upset, his mother calms him down with food. *Fatso* is a bit of a civil rights movie, calling for liberation of the fat people. DeLuise is shown at various stages in his life, struggling to lose weight, until, at the end of the movie when he's an old man, surrounded by his wife and daughters, he points to his wasting body and says, in effect, *See, I've finally lost weight!* And then he dies.

Gandolfini's weight, like many other actors', fluctuated over his career. He looks positively slim in *The Mexican*, huge in *Killing Them Softly*. He owned both a motorcycle and one of those Italian Vespa motor scooters—he said once the scooter made him look like "Shrek, you know, a big thing on a little thing?" He injured his knee on the scooter, delaying the shooting for the last season of *The Sopranos*. Ultimately, he had both knees replaced.

He put on weight rapidly in the last year or so of his life. In November 2012, about six months before his death, he described himself to Nicole Sperling of *The Los Angeles Times* as a "300-pound Woody Allen."

It wasn't as if Hollywood was the sort of place where people wouldn't notice, either. It's the home of mineral water–garglers, as we've said, a city famous for its obsession with fitness. Jim's defiance of all those norms was professionally fraught. He'd worried about it for years. In Susan Aston's apartment she has the big gold-leafed certificate for one of James's Screen Actors Guild Awards hanging, with a note from him giving her all the credit, the way he did. And it was signed, "The Fat Man."

Of course, the same thing happened to Marlon Brando at the end of his life, he became huge, almost spheroid. Maybe some stars are loved because they are fat—Fatty

Arbuckle, maybe—but most are loved in spite of being fat. Even now, in the midst of the obesity epidemic, we still have not crossed over into accepting that image of ourselves.

For Jim to act around America's body image prejudice—well, people talk about Dustin Hoffman in *Tootsie*, but a 300-pound romantic lead would be *acting*.

11.

Gotta Blue Moon in Your Eye

Leta Gandolfini, the younger of James's two older sisters, was on her way to the Boscolo Hotel Exedra from the airport when Michael found his father collapsed in the suite bathroom. Her flight from Paris had landed only a little while before. By the time she got to the Piazza della Repubblica, the paramedics were taking her brother to the hospital; Michael had handled the emergency, language barrier and all.

Marcy Wudarski caught the first flight out of Los Angeles to be with Michael. Gandolfini had been looking forward to Rome as a "boys' trip," just him and Michael, and Deborah Lin stayed in L.A., to be with Liliana Ruth, who was just over a year old. Tom Richardson was on the first flight from New York, to help expedite the body's return and the seemingly endless paperwork required by the Italian state. The paparazzi culture was, if anything, even more intrusive over there than it was here, and his first job would be handling the press.

Everybody was shocked. At fifty-one, Gandolfini seemed terribly young. The first speculations in the media were about drugs, but the autopsy dismissed that as a cause. Besides, a five-star hotel room you are sharing with your thirteen-year-old son after a day of sightseeing at the Vatican didn't really fit the John Belushi format.

When the cause of death, a massive heart attack, was announced, the next wave of speculation was about Jim's weight, and the *New York Post* story, based on a conversation with a hotel waiter, helped to push it. Many people took to social media to say they'd told us so. The *Post* story was exhibit A. The family pushed back through a spokesman, saying that not everything on the bill was as it seemed—in particular, the two piña coladas were nonalcoholic, for Michael. But it was true that Gandolfini's weight had shot up in the past year, possibly exacerbated by his second knee replacement, which had been done in late 2012.

There would be two funeral services: One small, for family and close friends, at the local funeral home in Park Ridge, in a modest white frame building with a big green awning and a little parking lot in front, not far from where the family's small Cape Cod had stood when Jim was growing up. The bigger service would be on the Upper West Side in Saint John the Divine, the largest church in New York City; HBO would handle all the details.

The funeral at Saint John's was a real New York event. There were media trucks and police barriers a couple of blocks on either side of the church's main portal. The nave inside was full, all the way to the doors, with lines of fans still left on the steps outside. HBO handed out press tips. Just before the service ended, New Jersey Governor Chris Christie, who'd entered through the side door with the other celebs, strode down the nave, through the public pews and out the main entrance, followed by a small spasm of much smaller aides.

The cast of *The Sopranos* was there, of course, writers from the show, actors Jim had worked with, everyone who was in the city or could make it came. All three of the women Jim had lived with, Marcy Wudarski, Deb Lin, and Lora Somoza, were there. Greg Antonacci, the actor who had complained about convertibles and cheeseburgers in the last episode of David Chase's *The Rockford Files*, was there, gray now but still thin and tight-lipped. Alec Baldwin, attending with his pregnant wife, Hilaria, managed to get into a dispute with a *Daily Mail* reporter over whether or not Hilaria had tweeted during the service; he launched a rant threatening the reporter with violence in a way many people took to be homophobic. That gave the assembled media something scandalous to worry over for a few days. Life goes on.

Another story was building on the Internet, about Gandolfini's estate. One of America's most successful representatives of the working class, James Gandolfini, had left behind an estate estimated to be worth $70 million, the reports said, but greedy Uncle Sam was going to seize almost half because of poor estate planning. It was an outrage, like all taxes on the wealthy. The story, which got its start on Web sites like Zero Hedge and other Wall Street–friendly outlets, was creating a minor storm. John Travolta had announced that he would make sure that Gandolfini's children were "taken care of"—did he say that because the government was putting them in the poorhouse? In the three weeks after Gandolfini's death, references to his estate tax bill became the most common Gandolfini-related topic on the Web, outrunning "fatty" mentions by a mile.

Exactly one month after Gandolfini's death, his lawyer, Roger Haber, reached out to *New York Times* financial reporter Paul Sullivan to spike the estate stories. Gandolfini's will was public, something rare for a celebrity, perhaps because Jim didn't see himself that way. But the will itself was only part of the story. There were appendices that allocated $1.6 million in bequests to friends, and family members were given percentages of the remaining estate; there may have been trusts set up to hold property, like his homes in New York and Tewksbury, that did not appear in the will. But Haber's main point was that the figure of $70 million, which came from a Web site that estimates the fortunes of celebrities, was wrong. The estate was worth more like $6 to $10 million.

Haber was miffed that *The Times* failed to exonerate him from the charge of poor estate planning—the article took for granted that we should all think about our estate planning as thoroughly as John Lennon did—but it made the Internet meme of Gandolfini's rough handling by the

IRS go away overnight. Friends who were in a position to know said Jim was very smart about money, but it was never his main focus. He told several of them that "I don't know where all my money goes."

He did, actually. Jamie's dad may have failed to make him see the real value of the change that fell out of his pockets on the sofa, but he and his two sisters both went on to have successful, productive careers. Money was there to support the family. Besides giving fellow cast members $33,000 apiece in the middle of *The Sopranos*, Jim set up funds to pay for the college education of some friends' kids, and he could be counted on in medical emergencies, too. He was generous with Lora Somoza. He took out a $7 million life insurance policy for Michael.

The money didn't disappear into paintings or antique cars or other personal property, the sorts of things Hollywood stars sometimes buy. Gandolfini liked art, but he wasn't a collector. The money was for family and friends. A lot of the people who sat in the family pews at Saint John's knew that firsthand. When they started to make Jim's generosities public, in the weeks after his death, it seemed almost too good to be true. It wasn't Antony reading Caesar's will or anything, but the record at least seemed refreshingly free of the privileged secrecy in which the 1 percent usually conduct such matters. Haber's need to tell the world that he'd acted appropriately in planning the estate was a sort of backhand proof of that.

As with *The Sopranos* pay negotiations, the money was

there, but it wasn't as much money as much more conventional careers command, and anyway money was not the ultimate measure. You didn't become the kind of actor Gandolfini was in order to get paid more than Frasier's dog.

The public service was as Catholic as it could be—Psalm 23, a choir singing "Ave Maria" during communion service, Lennie Loftin, Michael's godfather, reading from Revelations. Tom Richardson and Susan Aston eulogized their friend from the pulpit at Saint John the Divine, Susan saying he always had the "strength to keep his heart open." So did Deborah Lin, thanking her husband for "believing in me."

David Chase spoke, too.

David Chase had dreamed up Tony Soprano and then partnered with Gandolfini to bring him to life, but no one on Gandolfini's team ever thought of it as an equal partnership. "Chase was the creator, he was the showrunner," Mark Armstrong says. "He was the boss."

After Gandolfini's death, Chase refused to be interviewed about him; he reportedly felt any addition to his eulogy might be promoted as his last word on Gandolfini. So he couldn't be asked directly whether Tony Soprano was, in some way, David Chase, too.

He really isn't. Chase (the family name had been originally DeCesare, "of Caesar") was raised Italian in Newark, in a U-shaped, postwar development in Little Italy that has long since disappeared, replaced with newer versions of city renewal. His father owned a hardware store.

Chase wasn't even Catholic; he was raised a Protestant. He had Italian uncles and Italian aunts, but Italian macho the way Jersey guys think of it wasn't second nature to him. He'd call Maria Laurino, Jersey-born author of *Were You Always Italian?*, to make sure he was pronouncing the names of Italian-American dishes correctly. Chase left Jersey early, when he was still a kid, for California—he studied filmmaking at Stanford University, in Palo Alto. He never forgot the Garden State, but he wasn't circumscribed by it, either.

Chase was a writer on *The Rockford Files*, and wound up running *Northern Exposure*, a hit TV show in the mid-1990s. He was successful, by Hollywood standards. But everybody who knows him says he's a "glass-more-than-half-empty" kind of guy. At Silvercup Studios for HBO, he would occasionally interrupt meetings to say "I'm so fucking depressed" that another episode seemed impossible. He'd always make one, anyway, but expressions of creative joy were not in his line.

In earlier days, when he was working on *Northern Exposure*, Chase would come home to Santa Monica, where he lived with his wife, Denise, and fall on the floor to play Barbie dolls with their daughter, Michelle. Only, as an old friend who wrote three *Sopranos* scripts told journalist Peter Biskind, "he turned it into Perp-Walk Barbie—District

Attorney Barbie, Parole Officer Barbie. . . . I think he is a little obsessed with law and order. I think he gets angrier than most of us at the miscarriage of justice, at the injustice of the world."

In that sense, Chase was the opposite of Tony Soprano—he was on the side of the law. In real life, the law has far more Italian-Americans in its ranks than the Mafia does. Maria Laurino's brother Robert, for example, is a prosecutor in Essex County; for that matter, James's oldest sister, Johanna, runs the Family Court in Hackensack. Chase was careful to make several of his F.B.I. agents Italian-American, too.

It's more like crime has special meaning for Italian-Americans, because they have been blackened by American stories about the Mafia and because they have such high standards of community. Catholicism preaches a vision of civic responsibility that is modeled on the perfect family, each member defined by a series of mutual commitments to the other. Recreating that in a place as diverse as the United States is like herding cats: anybody who tries better have firm control of his temper.

Chase told Biskind that he and James were alike in that they both took out their frustrations on inanimate objects. But their active sense of injustice, which fed a smoldering anger, was another thing they had in common— like the "dark" undercurrent Chase says Hollywood detected in both men, and the work ethic that drove them both to never stop.

Chase's mother is, rather famously, the model for Livia Soprano, the operatic complainer whose emotional needs control much of her family. Livia was also the name of Augustus Caesar's wife, who killed him by painting the plums on his favorite tree with poison. DeCesare, indeed.

But Jim's mother was entirely different. She could make Jamie do things, of course; he once said he went to college just to "keep Mama happy." He was always trying to do that. He needed to reassure the woman whose desire to become a doctor had been thwarted by World War II that the life he had chosen would work out, as Lennie Loftin's story about their visit to Jim's beach house during the *Crimson Tide* shoot suggests. But their relationship was a kind of partnership—no doubt here, either, as to who was the junior partner—not some extended manipulation. Remember, when he was asked what he thought he'd inherited from his mom, Gandolfini said, "I don't know—introspective, depressed, a little judgmental, kind of smart about people."

Not a bad description, by all accounts, of David Chase.

The partners who made Tony Soprano were thinking about mother-son relationships from the beginning, but *The Sopranos* was essentially a long-form video meditation on growing up male. Manliness feels quite devalued today, and Italians often seem to feel this with a special intensity.

Chase wrote his eulogy to Gandolfini in the form of a letter addressed to Jim. After talking about how Jim's father and uncles had worked in construction, just as David's uncles had, Chase directly addresses Jim's doubts about his profession, his desire to be real, and most of all, his sense of masculinity:

The image of my uncles and father reminded me of something that happened between us one time. Because these guys were such men—your father and these men from Italy. And you were going through a crisis of faith about yourself and acting, a lot of things, were very upset. I went to meet you on the banks of the Hudson River, and you told me, you said, "You know what I want to be? I want to be a man. That's all. I want to be a man." Now, this is so odd, because you are such a man. You're a man in many ways many males, including myself, wish they could be a man. The paradox about you as a man is that I always felt personally, that with you, I was seeing a young boy. A boy about Michael's age right now. 'Cause you were very boyish. And about the age when humankind, and life on the planet are really opening up and putting on a show, really revealing themselves in all their beautiful and horrible glory. And I saw you as a boy—as a sad boy, amazed and confused and loving and amazed by all that. And that was all in your eyes. And that was why, I think, you were a great actor: because of that boy who was inside. He was a child reacting. Of course you were intelligent, but it was a child reacting, and your reactions were often childish. And by that, I mean they were preschool, they were premanners, they were preintellect. They were just simple emotions, straight and pure. And I think your talent is that you can take in the immensity of humankind and the universe, and shine it out to the rest of us like a huge bright light. And I believe that only a pure soul, like a child, can do that really well. And that was you.

You can't help but think that the boy who was voted "Class Flirt" at Park Ridge High School must have had some sort of special charm—it's actually not easy to flirt and fail to offend when you're a teenager. "Oh, he was always a magnet for women," T.J. Foderaro told me; Susan Aston said, "Women were always very attracted to James." Even as Gandolfini flopped so terribly at summer stock tryouts back in 1980, Mark Di Ionno told me he nevertheless found a girl, and made an annoyed Di Ionno cool his heels for a while until they'd said their good-byes. More than one buddy fell out with Jim for a time over a wandering girlfriend.

And yet, there is that image of Wudarski, Somoza, and Lin all sitting within a few yards of one another in the pews of Saint John the Divine. Maybe they felt, like his other friends, that Jim never left you, exactly. Once you're family, you're always family. Always there for each other.

Of course, there was that "enduring sex symbol" thing. Woody Allen once said that Humphrey Bogart was short and kind of ugly, but as long as he had women like Lauren

Bacall or Ingrid Bergman falling in love with him on the screen, nobody noticed. We saw Tony Soprano with lots of beautiful women on TV. They didn't seem to mind that he was balding and developing a paunch. Why should anyone else?

Before he died, Gandolfini had several projects in various states of completion. He was hoping to narrate documentaries, and he was beginning to work as a producer. He was reading more and more books "mostly for plot," he said. In 2012 he produced HBO's *Hemingway & Gellhorn*, about the novelist and his journalist wife during the Spanish Civil War, after he turned down the part of Hemingway.

But his big project in his final year was *Enough Said*, a movie written and directed by Woody Allen protégé Nicole Holofcener. It would be Gandolfini's first romantic comedy, and only his second romantic lead in a feature film, after Guskin and Jennings's *Kiddie Ride/Down the Shore*. *Enough Said* was being prepared for a 2014 release when Gandolfini died, but Fox Searchlight put it into an accelerated postproduction schedule and premiered it in September 2013.

Enough Said stars Julia Louis-Dreyfus as Eva, a divorced masseuse in Los Angeles who stumbles into a bittersweet romance with a divorced TV librarian while unwittingly becoming good friends with his former wife (Catherine Keener), a successful poet.

The genre form is romantic comedy, but *Enough Said*

swerves from rom-com conventions. For one thing, it can be scathing toward its female characters. Eva's inability to set boundaries between her love life, family life, and friendships is the source of the plot's conflict; as Albert, Gandolfini is quite aware of his flaws, but trying, with extraordinary dignity, to risk love again. He winds up, rather amazingly, as the only adult in the film.

The film was treated as a posthumous triumph; *New York Times* movie critic A. O. Scott called *Enough Said* "one of the best-written American film comedies in recent memory and an implicit rebuke to the raunchy, sloppy spectacles of immaturity that have dominated the genre in recent years."

Jim had his second knee replacement surgery shortly before shooting, and for a while was getting around the set with a cane. He was working on a project full of women, in a genre aimed largely at women, out among the expensive bungalows of Malibu. It would be hard to get farther from Guinea Gulch and the pack of boys who held sway at *The Sopranos*.

"He was very nervous about playing a romantic lead," Holofcener told me. "He asked me to come into his trailer because, he said, he wanted to be sure I knew what I was getting into. And so I follow him in, he asks me if I'm ready, and he takes off his shirt.

"My first thought was, dude, I know what you look like. But I told him he was fine, I thought he looked great, that was what I wanted. Then he had the confidence to go on."

She says there was no indication that *Enough Said* would be his last role. "You knew he had had a really risky past, with alcohol and everything," Holofcener says, "but he's there, he's very alive, you don't think he's going to die. It was a huge shock.

"You know we had fights," she adds. "Directors and actors have fights. There were things he found hard to do. There was one scene, his big confrontation and declaration scene with Julia, and he said, 'You got me crying like a bitch in the kitchen!' I just never forgot that. Like, the place where you cry makes a difference. 'You got me crying like a bitch *in the kitchen*!' We fought about it for a while, but I just kept at him. And then he did it, and he was great."

Enough Said promised to be the most commercially successful of the five feature films Holofcener has directed (she's also worked as a director on *Sex and the City*, *Six Feet Under*, and Amy Poehler's *Parks and Recreation*). Holofcener says she was surprised when Gandolfini told her that he knew her other films, and liked them. He gave her the impression that he especially liked her attitude toward class in films like *Friends With Money*.

It doesn't take a lot of imagination to think *Enough Said* meant a lot to Gandolfini. Here he was, playing an adult at last, a kind of Mitch—only in this movie, Mitch was the lead. His character roles had finally grown up. Sooner or later, we all do—it's the play actor in us that never does.

"He had a real thing going with the prop lady on the

production," Holofcener remembers. "She was very thin, a kind of California girl, into health foods and everything, and on the day we were to shoot the scene where he greets Julia at his door in pajama bottoms, [the prop lady] wore blue jeans and this tiny orange tube top. Jim was kidding her about it. You know, like 'What're you hiding,' silly jokes. And Jim is wearing this black T-shirt, it's actually the shirt I picked out for him to wear.

"But my cinematographer starts saying, 'Oh no, I can't shoot you, darling, you are like a wall of black to me, I can't do it.' And Jim says he knows what to do, give him a second and he'll change.

"So he goes to his trailer, and when he comes back, he's wearing the tiny orange tube top, and the prop lady is in his tent of a black shirt, and it was just hilarious. You had to see it—I have a picture of it, on my cell phone, which absolutely no one will ever see—I think that's just for me.

"Jim was like that. That's what I'll always remember."

But Gandolfini's posthumous career didn't end with *Enough Said*. In March of 2013, immediately after wrapping his first performance as a romantic lead in a major release, he plunged into a project that took him back once more to the working-class, hard-bitten suburbs of New York City and the criminal culture they spawn.

Based on a script by novelist Dennis Lehane (*Mystic River, Shutter Island*), *Animal Rescue* is about a pit bull pup found in a trash container outside a mobbed-up bar in Brooklyn. Due out in 2014 from Fox Searchlight, *Animal Rescue* was filmed in the final months of Gandolfini's life (he was on the set of *Animal Rescue* when *Burt Wonderstone* was premiering). Tom Hardy and Noomi Rapace play the leads, but the whole set, according to *The Los Angeles Times* in March 2013, buzzed with anticipation for the big star—who got there and ate lunch with the grippers and gaffes instead of retreating to his private trailer. The *Times* said Jim and the crew would gab about "everything under the sun, including dogs, a big theme in the film."

"There was no star thing with Jim," says Belgian director Michaël Roskam, whose first feature film, *Bullhead*, also about animals caught up in a criminal subculture, was nominated for Best Foreign Language Film in 2012. Roskam is young—born in 1972. He studied painting at the St. Lucas Academy of Fine Art in Brussels and worked for a time as a journalist before going into filmmaking. As I write this, *Animal Rescue* is still in post-production, lying in pieces on a table for Roskam to assemble. But it should be in theaters either a little before or after this book is published.

"I, of course, didn't know what to expect when I met him," Roskam says, but he quickly picked up on Gandolfini's unusual attitude toward his celebrity. "It was almost like he would try to hide among all the people, that was how he tried to disappear. And it was an irony, you know, that he was always the tallest guy in the room. He could not hide."

In *Animal Rescue,* Gandolfini plays the former owner of the bar, uncle to Hardy's character, who is both nostalgic about once running the place and resentful of his demotion to mere bartender. With very little time between roles to prepare, Jim was characteristically dubious about capturing the part—Roskam remembers him suggesting another actor, true to form. And then, on the first or second day of filming, Hardy and Gandolfini were asked to do a key, very emotional scene almost from a cold start. Roskam had to convince Jim he could do it. Gandolfini kept asking, "Are you serious?"

"He was great, of course," Roskam says. Like Holofcener, Roskam thought Gandolfini's physical presence was important; when, during casting, producers worried that the milieu was too much like that of *The Sopranos,* he'd give them the option of hiring Bryan Cranston of *Breaking Bad.* But Jim was always his first choice.

"I don't know if you are going to deal with this in your book, but Jim suffered from that, from his inability to get away from the role of Tony," Roskam says. But there was a difference now.

"I experienced him as a man who could deal with his insecurities," Roskam continues. "You know, we are all insecure. It's how you handle it.

"We need that vulnerability to make art. But that means an artist lives scared. You have to dedicate yourself to being vulnerable if you're going to go on making serious art, not just doing what is comfortable. And I thought Jim saw this and had learned how to deal with it."

"Living scared" is a pretty good description of an actor's life—a description both Harold Guskin and David Chase would endorse. Roskam describes Gandolfini as someone who was almost comfortable with that psychological state. Susan Aston told Jim in his last year that he would always be able to work as long as he wanted, which for an actor is a rare success. Other friends say he was beginning to accept the truth of that.

And he was growing out of Tony. Roskam says he didn't even look like Tony anymore.

By the time of *Animal Rescue*, Jim was much heavier than he had ever been. Though he rarely spoke about his health, he had to know something about how delicate it might be. The two knee surgeries must have been preceded by tests to see if his heart was strong enough to endure them. Anyway, the long convalescence may well have exacerbated his weight problem. Roskam recalled one incident during a basement shoot for *Animal Rescue* in Brooklyn when Jim, wearing a leather jacket and surrounded by a large crew and hot lights in a cramped space, complained that he was short of breath. He had to step outside.

Roskam says he was briefly worried. But when Gandolfini came back after a few minutes, he did the scene perfectly. He was, after all, just fifty-one.

Gandolfini was undergoing more than just a physical change in those last months. After *Enough Said,* he was learning how to disappear into his roles again. He had a future, and it wasn't as the guy who ambled down his driveway to pick up *The Star-Ledger* in a polar bear's bathrobe every week.

He was becoming an elder in his tribe, a Hollywood hand.

"I think we had a strong professional relationship that had evolved, in the end, to be a real professional friendship," Roskam says. "And the reason I say that is that Jim told me at the end of shooting that he was planning his trip to Rome, and he thought he might expand it, you know, see a little bit of everything. And he said he'd decided to spend three days in Brussels, where I'm from, and he wanted me to recommend good hotels, maybe suggest a friend or two who could show him around. It was very sweet."

Roskam says the "business side" of making films in the United States is much more prevalent than it is in Europe, and he was finding his way around inside the much bigger system over here. And Gandolfini seemed to understand that.

"He gave me a photograph, a long horizontal photograph of the back of the Hollywood sign, which is all covered with graffiti, you know," Roskam says. "And you can glimpse, just barely, Los Angeles through the spaces between the letters. I had told him I might move to Los

Angeles and I think he was giving me this present as a kind of warning, that this is what the real Hollywood was like—you know, don't be fooled by the facade, don't be seduced by what it seems to be. He wrote me a note in his own hand that said so. I thought that was a wonderful gift. A man who can give a present like that, which is beautiful in itself but also carries a message, is an artist."

Index

Photos from the photo section are indicated as *p1*, *p2*, *p3* respectively